"Woodstock without any politics, without a commitment to self-defense of the nation is a shuck. A tin-pan alley rip-off. When they say, 'Hey, man, politics is not where it's at,' what they are really saying is, 'Don't bug me, I wanna keep all my dough and the status quo.' Peter Max is Consciousness III. Peter Max loves the planet earth. Peter Max paints designs for bathtowels sold by gas stations across the country that pollute that very planet. The whole scene of hip fashions is not the scene of this book. Woodstock Nation is not the Woodstock movie. Woodstock Nation is at war with the Pig Empire; the Woodstock movie is a weapon in the arsenal of the pigs, designed to defeat the nation by rendering it impotent. People at Warner Brothers brag how they purged the Nation from the movie. Most of the stuff in this book ended up on the cutting room floor." —Abbie Hoffman, from the special Epilogue for this edition of *Woodstock Nation*

"Funny, intelligent, and outrageous."
—*Los Angeles Times*

"Remarkable...liberally salted with those words that Mother used to wash your mouth out for using."
—*Washington Post*

WOODSTOCK NATION
was originally published by Random House, Inc.

Also by Abbie Hoffman

Fuck the System

Revolution for the Hell of It*

*Published by POCKET BOOKS

WOODSTOCK NATION

A Talk-Rock Album

by Abbie Hoffman

PUBLISHED BY POCKET BOOKS NEW YORK

Large sections of the songs that appear on the following
pages have appeared in various underground newspapers serviced by Liberation New Service: 30, 40, 48;
"Che's Last Letter" appeared in The Realist, "Hard
Rain's Already Fallin" in Woodstock Festival program.
The "Outline Yippie! Movie" and "To Anita" were
written in late 1968. The rest was done in five
days after Woodstock.

Art stands against history, withstands history which has been the history of oppression, for art subjects reality to laws other than the established ones: to the laws of the Form which creates a different reality — negation of the established one even where art depicts the established reality. But in its struggle with history, art subjects itself to history: history enters the definition of art and enters into the distinction between art and pseudo-art. Thus it happens that what was once art becomes pseudo-art. Previous forms, styles and qualities, previous modes of protest and refusal cannot be recaptured in or against a different society.

Herbert Marcuse, *Repressive Tolerance*

The real meaning of revolution is not a change in management, but a change in man. This change we must make in our own lifetime and not for our children's sake, for the revolution must be born of joy and not sacrifice.

Cohn-Bendit, *Obsolete Communism,*
A Left-Wing Alternative

We are moving towards a conscious community of artists and lovers who live together, work together, share all things — smoke dope together, dance and fuck together, and spread the word together every way we can — through our dress, our freedom of movement, our music and dance, our economy, our human social forms, through our every breath on this planet.

John Sinclair, 1964

PHOTO CREDITS

Ken Regan — Pages 16 & 17, 90, 93, 103, 148 & 149
Benno Friedman — 154
Christopher Cerf — 72
Magdelene Sinclair — 62 & 63
Don Snyder — 70
David Upright — 49, 134
Elliot Landy — 108
UPI — 9, 27 (3), 37, 84, 117

DESIGN — CONCERT HALL PUBLICATIONS

Dedicated to LENNY BRUCE

About ten years ago when I was into psychology stuff, I bumped into a guy I knew from high school days. He was an undertaker in Boston and he asked me if I knew anything about suicide.

"Well like what?" I said, in that clinical noncommittal voice I had mastered.

"Cause everytime we get a suicide, it's the weirdest thing but they always got this grin on their faces. No matter how they go: hanging, gas or whatever, they always got this certain grin."

"You sure that's true?"

"No shit, we even got a name for it in the trade it's called 'THE SHIT-EATIN GRIN' and every one of the fuckers got it...."

"What do you do about it? Like how come nobody but undertakers knows about it?"

"Are you kiddin? We couldn't talk about a thing like that, not in our position. We even have to change the expressions on their face. You know, make em look more serious. They fight like hell even if they're dead. We have to use special needles to relax their face muscles and finally we get em lookin serious enough for the funeral. I mean you just could never bury a guy with a shit-eatin grin, no sir."

This story is for you, Lenny, from all the
Yippies

Song Titles

Foreplay

Knowing WHERE is as important as
knowing WHAT or WHO, so why don't I
introduce myself with some thoughts on
environment. Why don't we begin to

construct the map. Two days ago (the day after the whole Woodstock thing was over)* I realized I had badly misjudged the event. See, if you consider the event as a festival in the traditional sense of the word, like the Monterey Pop Festival or the Newport Folk Festival, then three people getting killed, a few thousand injuries, lack of food and water and hundreds of bum trips lead you to draw bad conclusions (or "bad vibes" as they say in the rock biz) about what happened. If, on the other hand, you consider that the sheer number of beautiful people struggling against the inclement weather, and basic needs of survival, turned the festival into a Nation dedicated to victory, then the bummers get put in quite a different perspective.

I'm a great believer in the notion of subjective environment. McLuhan says, "Environment is like a plastic dome inside another plastic dome." We can vaguely see out into other people's worlds but everything is clouded by the walls around us, the walls that we construct in our heads.

Sometime about 3:00 a.m. Sunday morning (or so I'm told since nothing that happened in WOODSTOCK NATION goes by Fascist Clock-Time), the plastic dome came crashing down on me. It might have been the green tab, the red one, the blue, the Darvon, four joints, no food, hash, no sleep for five days, witnessing the hundreds who had dragged their bodies through the hospital we had set up, the thousands waiting outside the gate to get treatment for bad trips, or the fact that I tried to ball every woman I ever wanted in one day and they all said no.

*I had to beat it out a day before the festival ended but the high point everyone agrees was Saturday night when the greatest music event in history occurred. Sunday, except for Jimi Hendrix bringing up the sun, was anticlimactic — at least that's what my friends say.

4

Whatever it was I had a bummer. One of those rare acid trips when everything caves in. I learned enough shit from it, though, that maybe it wasn't such a bummer after all. All I can say is, man, I took a heavy trip!

Most of this book is about that trip and afterward or before. It culminated with a battle on stage with The Who. The battle symbolizes my amity-enmity attitude toward that particular rock group and the whole rock world in general. Clearly I love their music and sense in it the energy to liberate millions of minds. On the other hand, I feel compelled to challenge their role in the community, to try and crack their plastic dome. It's a different plastic dome than running around setting up hospitals in the hills of the NATION and trying to wreck the government that claims it owns our land. Also, it's quite a different plastic dome than the one sitting about forty feet from the front of the stage, forgoing water, food, sleep, shelter from the rain and lots more just to BE THERE when it all came blasting out of those ever-lovin amplifiers. The za-za world of rock is almost entirely an uptown plastic dome. Up at Woodstock it meant living at the Concord hotel or the Holiday Inn in Liberty and buzzing in stoned out of your head in a helicopter. It meant being hustled under guard to a secluded pavilion to join the other aristocrats who run the ROCK EMPIRE. There one could dig the whole spaced-out scene and dine on California grapes and champagne, just forty yards below the Field Hospital where a thousand screaming freak-outs were happening and cats with barbed wire through their feet were moaning on the cots.

Yeah, there sure were a lot of plastic domes floating around and this record album I'm writing makes an attempt to smash a few including my own beautiful thick-sculled one. Mark Twain once wrote that the only people that should use the word "we" are editors, kings, and persons with tapeworms. Yet there is 5 a way of integrating your own ego trip with a sense of community, with a concept of the "we." I feel a sense of this most strongly in these massive events, in what Artaud refers to as the "festival of the streets." I felt it in the WOODSTOCK NATION and just one year ago today in the streets of Chicago. Chicago is the capital of PIG NATION. There the pigs didn't wear bell-bottoms and peace symbols, they wore riot helmets and gas masks. The helicopters brought in troops and machine guns, not guitar players and drums. Last year I had a fight with a tank on Michigan Avenue, not a battle with a rock group at the foot of People Hill. In lots of ways the two trips were similar but in many ways they were not and those differences are what thrash about in my plastic dome as I try to sort out my thoughts.

I'm trying to write the same kind of non-book in the same kind of non-way as last year. Lying on the floor in an office of the publisher, I'm flying high on adrenalin, excitement, no sleep, rock music* and pot.

*I am absorbing the following while I write:
    Canned Heat — "Hallelujah"
    Soundtrack from "Easy Rider"
    Blind Faith (horny cover)
    The Band — "Big Pink"
    MC 5 — "Kick Out the Jams "
    (motherfucker edition)
    Creedence Clearwater Revival
    Moby Grape — "Grape Jam"
    Bob Dylan — "Nashville Skyline"
    Rolling Stones — "Their Satanic
    Majesties Request"
    Big Brother and the Holding Company —
    "Cheap Thrills"
    Jimi Hendrix Experience —
    "Axis: Bold as Love"
and of course "Tommy" by The Who. If I hear anything good I'll get it in somehow, but, dig, it's hard quotin words from records. Not only are they shouted, slurred and jiggled, but the laws on quotin' records are a drag and the publisher will take some chances but he wouldn't run the risk of getting sued by a record company.

Using what I can find lying around, I write out every word by hand. The book is drawn and sung as much as it is written in an attempt to recapture the mess that was up in WOODSTOCK and out there in the PIG NATION. I also try to open the door to the mess that is in my head and yours. The medium is the mess. It has to be finished quick in order to have some bread for The TRIAL* that begins next month in Chicago and to help build a campaign to get our brother John Sinclair and a lot of other political prisoners out of jail.

During the past few years I have straddled the line between "the movement" and "the community," between "the left" and "the hip," between the world of "the street" and the world of "media." I have doubts that I can go on balancing these forces in my head much longer.

I emerged exhausted, broke and bleeding from the WOODSTOCK NATION. It was an awesome experience but one that made me have a clearer picture of myself as a cultural revolutionary — not a cultural nationalist, for that would embrace a concept of hip capitalism which I reject — and not a political revolutionary either. Political revolution leads people into support for other revolutions rather than having them get involved in making their own. Cultural revolution requires people to change the way they live and act in the revolution rather than passing judgments on how the other folks are proceeding. The cultural view creates outlaws, politics breeds organizers.

Certainly some jabs will be taken here at my cousin revolutionaries, especially those identified in the

*Actually I have four trials coming up but when I refer to "the trial" I mean the trial for conspiracy with intent to incite riots during the Democratic Convention in Chicago. The trial begins September twenty-fourth and people who wish to help us can send bread to the Committee to Defend the Conspiracy, 28 East Jackson Boulevard, Chicago, Illinois, 60604.

mind of the public as the "New Left," but these are meant in the spirit of free interchange and to get a sense of the fluidity and contradictions in the total revolution going on today. I feel certain I have emerged a cultural revolutionary concerned with building and defending the new NATION that gave us a glimpse of its beauty on the shores of White Lake in the Catskill mountains.

When I appear in the Chicago courtroom, I want to be tried not because I support the National Liberation Front — which I do — but because I have long hair. Not because I support the Black Liberation Movement, but because I smoke dope. Not because I am against a capitalist system, but because I think property eats shit. Not because I believe in student power, but that the schools should be destroyed. Not because I'm against corporate liberalism, but because I think people should do whatever the fuck they want, and not because I am trying to organize the working class, but because I think kids should kill their parents. Finally, I want to be tried for having a good time and not for being serious. I'm not angry over Vietnam and racism and imperialism. Naturally, I'm against all that shit but I'm *really* pissed cause my friends are in prison for dope and cops stop me on the street cause I have long hair. I'm guilty of a conspiracy, all right. Guilty of creating liberated land in which we can do whatever the fuck we decide. Guilty of helping to bring the WOODSTOCK NATION to the whole earth. Guilty of trying to overthrow the motherfuckin senile government of the U.S. of A. I just thought you ought to know where my head was at, PIG NATION. Just thought I'd let you know what I mean when I say, "I'm just doin my thing."

Enough of this bullshit! Light up your joint, inhale and proceed to the next song.

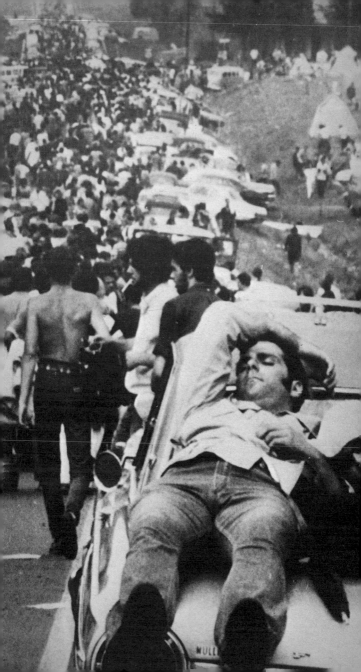

Landing a Man on the Earth without the Help of Norman Mailer

When I finished *Revolution for the Hell of It* in three days the first thing I did was fly up to Provincetown to armwrestle Norman Mailer. I sure looked a sight coming up that road barefoot, my Medusa-like long hair flying mad all over my grinnin puss. I knew my Chicago battle-crazy face was staring out at Mailer from the center of *The New York Times* Magazine Section that had been delivered that morning. It was some feat writing the book that quick, quicker by weeks than even Mailer who was damn fast and damn fuckin good even if he was getting a little too clinical and even though his Negro maid answered the door. He was the best all right, the best writer in *their* NATION. In WOODSTOCK NATION there are no writers — only poet-warriors.

WOODSTOCK NATION is built on ELECTRICITY. It is our energy, music, politics, school, religion, play, battleground and our sensuality. I hesitate only in using the word Morality, for Morality means soul and ELECTRICITY lacks soul but so too does this

10

wooden pen I scratch against the yellow pad. Morality rests in God's imagination and if we see ourselves as gods I guess we alone make those choices. Moral decisions never rest in our tools, be they electricity or pencils, flowers or guns.

I suppose Mailer also had such thoughts; after all, he has a good mind and is always testing his environment. In the year following Chicago, I too tried to experiment: a book and a half, three quick movies, one to design and edit, the other two to improvise-act in, and lots more to get absorbed into like "The Wild Bunch," "Savage Seven" (brilliant sleeper about bikers and Indians joining together to rip off a fat capitalist named Fillmore), "Midnight Cowboy," and of course, the almost perfect propaganda film, "Easy Rider." I also did a unique Yippie calendar, ten or so street theatre events, wasted time battling SDS, gave about seventy speech-performances, had hepatitis and almost died, flew about eighty thousand miles, spent a lot of time in court with my lawyer Jerry Lefcourt, helped paint the apartment, take out the garbage and cooked a lot (Women's Liberation take note in case you get pissed later when I use the word "chick"). In between I managed to write about thirty articles, mostly under other names, for the underground press, and a few children's stories. I founded the Movement Speakers' Bureau — a very good idea — and helped to hustle bread and spread the word on the conspiracy trial. I took about twenty acid trips, fucked about 856 times and did a few things that only the FBI knows about and lots of other stuff they don't. I managed to get busted only ten times and face a possible thirty-seven years or so in prison. I also quit smoking of which I am proudest of all. It ain't been too busy a year, but maybe that's cause I was zonked with the hep for three months, so for a nine-month year it ain't bad, especially since the in-fighting between movement groups and factions had reached grating proportions. I suppose all this energy results from being an anarchist, Jewish, bottle-fed, stubborn, beautiful, white, spoiled brat, dedicated, male, young, old, optimistic, Sagittarius, schmuck, revolutionist, communist, god, self-destructive, egotistical, horny, show-off, paranoid-schizophrenic, naive, fucked-up, big-mouth, not serious, brilliant, honest Yippie leader and non-leader and a whole lot more from Concord, Mass., and the Bronx, New York.*

Well, anyway, there I was on my way to see Mailer for an arm-wrestling contest, something at which I was pretty damn good considering I am a light-weight. Three months later I was to fight a draw with MIT Professor of Communications, Jerome Lettvin, on his television show in Boston. That was some trip. He weighed about twice as much as me and smoked a cigar while he grunted and I swore out phrases at him in Yiddish like *alta kaka* as I strained. Paul Krassner sort of refereed. I was on acid and had just driven a car through the Concord Bridge parking lot fence. Lettvin's wife, who teaches gym classes for early-morning viewers, cheered him on, and my two kids, age eight and six, cheered me on. It was a draw and each of us developed a certain measure of respect for the other. I saw this cat debate Leary and thought that battle was a draw. I figured I'd lay the professor out by doing whatever the fuck came along, just act out answers instead of playing interviewer word-game mish-mash.

> LETTVIN: *(Alta kaka voice)* Why do you insist on calling policemen pigs?
> ABBIE: *(Spoiled brat)* Cause on TV we can't call them cocksuckers.
> LETTVIN: *(For the third time)* Yes, yes, I've heard that, but what is this revolution going to accomplish?
> ABBIE: *(Smiles and kicks over the table, smashing two ashtrays and making a general mess)*
> LETTVIN: *(Excited)* I knew it! Violence! Violence! You'll never win.

*Each descriptive phrase appeared in somebody's review of me. I wonder what critics see when they get up in the morning and look in the mirror.

ABBIE: *(Pulling out a ten dollar bill and holding it up)* Wanna bet ten bucks?

LETTVIN: *(Reaching for the bill)* Let me see that.

ABBIE: *(Pulling it back and ripping it slowly into pieces)* Hey man, we've already won.

Well, I never cracked Norman Mailer's defenses, never even saw him that day, but when I glimpsed the way he lived an all I wasn't interested any more in arm-wrestling him. It was sort of the feeling I had later when I told one of his campaign aides in the primary that Norman should swim the East River to Brooklyn, Mao-style, to make the point that if he were elected he would clean the river so everyone could swim in it by 1974 (which, incidentally, could be done). That aide just gave me this Eugene McCarthy-liberal look that spelled C-R-A-Z-Y. Guess me and that bit just ain't his scene. Like booze and Negro maids ain't mine.

Anyway, Mailer is off writing his book on the space program for $1,000,000 for *Life* magazine, while I try to sort out the most remarkable event in *our* history (as opposed to *their* history), the creation of WOODSTOCK NATION. It was a phenomenal burst of human energy and spirit that came and went like a tidal wave up there in White Lake, Bethel, Woodstock, Aquarian Exposition, Music Festival, Happening, Monster, or whatever you called the fuckin thing. I took a trip to our future. That's how I saw it. Functional anarchy, primitive tribalism, gathering of the tribes. Right on! What did it all mean? Sheet, what can I say, brother, it blew my mind out. It blew it in the way I guess Mailer's mind is now gettin blown out in Houston, Texas, while he tries to rationalize the meaning of men walking around on the moon. To each his own cup of TEA.

If I had to sum up the totality of the Woodstock experience I would say it was the first attempt to land a man on the earth. It took an awful lot of people to pull if off, but pull it off we did. Welcome to the Aquarian Age.

13

Thorns of the Flower Children

Once upon a time, about a generation ago, right after the thirteen-thousand-seven-hundred-and-sixty-fourth demonstration against the war in Vietnam, young people started to congregate in an area of San Francisco known as the Haight-Ashbury. They were sick of being programmed by an educational system void of excitement, creativity and sensuality. A system that channeled human beings like so many laboratory rats with electrodes rammed up their asses into a highly mechanized maze of class rankings, degrees, careers, neon supermarkets, military-industrial complexes, suburbs, repressed sexuality, hypocrisy, ulcers and psychoanalysts. The world they came from was a world of Double Speak. A world where Lyndon Johnson and his fabulous wife Lady Bird sat in their Miami-modern ranch house, drank their bourbon, and led the nation in a marathon game of Scrabble. The victor, naturally, would donate the winnings to his or her favorite charity.

"Mah fellow Pigs, this land of ours is the most peace-loving nation in the history of the world. This government stands for peace. It does not believe social change can come about through violence. Oink-oink."

Saigon, Vietnam: Colonel James Rivers, a veteran of World War II, Korea, and now in Vietnam, stated that the American fighting man never had it so good as in Vietnam. Just back from supervising a raid in the Mekong Delta in which over 5,000 of the enemy were killed in three days of heavy fighting, Rivers admitted, "This is the only war in history where the fighting man can sleep in a warm bed, eat a good breakfast, take a helicopter ride to battle, pause for a lunch break and return to the base in a

helicopter in time for supper and a look at the day's fighting on the evening's telecast. Vietnam is the first commuter war," he explained.

And, when the game was over, Latin America, "our partners in progress," was selected as PIG NATION'S favorite charity.

Rio de Janeiro, Brazil: Top sources in the U.S. Foreign Aid Program revealed today that of the 25,000 tons of meat shipped to Brazil under the Alliance for Progress, 85 per cent ended up in the hands of wealthy ranch owners.

Meanwhile back on the ranch, the Boob-Tube was filling our heads with all kinds of cotton-candy news.

New York, New York: WPIX-TV (Channel 11) was reprimanded today by the Federal Communications Commission for showing pictures of maneuvers in Fort Belvoir, Virginia and labeling them Central Highlands and Danang. They also were accused of showing old footage depicting crowd scenes from Budapest and

renaming them Prague. When reached, the station had no comment.

So the kids had heard a lot of stuff and had made their minds up. They saw their fathers disappear behind the corn flakes box and hurry off to his other life in a distant land called DOWNTOWN. On weekends they saw them mowing the lawn with a dumblooking gadget that broke down more than it worked. They saw them load up station wagons with golf clubs and run off to stand in line for five hours to have fun (?) on the golf course running around in Bermuda shorts and silly little shoes. They heard from their mothers over and over again about being *respectable* and *responsible* and, above all, *reasonable*. They would say things like:

What's going on is simply terrible. You never can be too white... What's the matter with kids these days? When I was your age... I think you'll straighten out once you get into college... Your views would be O.K. if only you would cut your hair...

They monopolized the TV set with Bob Hope, baseball games, situation comedies about people like them and of course Ed Sullivan. They liked to "keep up" so they read *Time* Magazine and the N.Y. *Times* on Sunday. When some politician came on TV they would say things like, "That fellah makes damn good sense." It sure was a drag. If there ever was a Desolation Row it climbed into the front seat of the Oldsmobile on Monday morning, checked its passport and headed DOWNTOWN and not the one that Petula Clark sang about, no sir not that DOWNTOWN. Downtown Desolation Row is Wall Street not Times Square. The old men get their rocks off in the Stock Exchange, not in the balcony of the Apollo or the Guild or even the De Mille or Loew's State....

And the music told it over and over:

See my daddy in bed a-dyin,
See his hair turnin gray,
He's been workin and slavin his life away,

He's been workin, workin, work-work.

The work that the kids saw around them was so odious, so boring, so worthless that they came to regard WORK as the only dirty four-letter word in the English language.

So the kids took off for the hills of Vermont and the deserts of New Mexico and the slums of the Lower East Side and lots of places in between. Millions more took the trip. Millions ran away with flowers in their hair. Maybe they just took off for a coupla days, maybe they took off forever. Some even died on the road. But they took off from Desolation Row every time they snuck a joint in the afternoon when Mom was down at the laundromat.

The ones who made it were tough. Tough as all hell. Like bare feet that had crawled through glass-jagged streets like Tenth Street and the Haight. People that can keep their minds together amid slum chaos.

> See that girl, barefoot (doeeyoumoo)
> Whistlin and a-singin
> She's a carryin on
> Laughin in her eyes, dancin in her feet,
> She a (neonwhirrwhirrmoo)
> And she can live on the street.
>
> Grateful Dead

A new culture with psychedelic wings and big ears for hearing heavy sounds was perched up on the telephone wires. "Hey Prudence, come on out and pla-aaay." "Hey brother! Hey sister!" "Break on through to the other side." "Turn on, tune in, drop out," sang the Leary singers and although the parents were leery of Reverend Tim the kids weren't leery at all. Not one bit.

Then it happened. PIG NATION came to collect its kids, some sad-looking, tweed-suited, boney dude named George and a bitchy wife he called Delilah. Behind them was this huge motherfuckin steel-and-chrome Moloch called BIG BUSINESS. George had a straight jacket and Delilah, you guessed it, a pair of scissors. BIG BUSINESS had the biggest mouth you ever saw and loads of teeth, flat like cows' teeth for grinding. It was said that Moloch regurgitated his food. You would have believed anything if you had seen him comin.

So what did the kids do? Well, everybody made up stories. Like they went to Bellevue, or went home or got killed in the cellar on Avenue B, or went back to school, or went to the country. In the land of the hippies everybody was always "going to the country" even if they were already there.

The cops didn't buy the peace-and-flower shit, no sir, a lot of folks mostly liberals bought that crap but not the cops, hell no. They didn't see the "beautiful people," the "gentle generation," they saw commie-drug-addict-sex-crazy-dirty-homosexual-nigger-draft-card-burner-runaway-spoiled-brats. What they also saw was *their* kids, for they too were letting their hair grow a little longer and putting up those weird posters that stared out at them as they cruised past the local head shop. And that music! Why did it have to be so loud? It wasn't just the cops though, cause cops are part of a paid army and soldiers in a non-revolutionary force take orders. So people higher up, even if they didn't scream it as they charged in a flying wedge, felt the pressure and thought it. "Kill those fuckin hippies, my kid'll be with em next." "Get em quick; before you know it they'll be in Chicago throwing bags of shit." "Isn't it about time we had some LAW and ORDER?" Which is simply a more polite way of saying "Kill those fuckin hippies."

Hippies took a lot of crap. Illegal busts of crash pads and communes in the Lower East Side. Arbitrary curfews in Cambridge. Signs saying "Barefoot People Keep Out" and "We Do Not Serve Hippies Here" in the Big Sur area of California. Tear gas raids on

Haight-Ashbury. Heavy fighting at a music festival in Palm Springs and, at that crossroad of all movements, Telegraph Avenue, pitched battles over a people's park. Here the Berkeley Pigs earned their nickname well, as they pumped tear gas and buckshot into kids and killed a twenty-five-year-old long-hair watching from a roof. His name was and still is James Rector. You ought to take your hat off when you hear his name.

WOODSTOCK NATION wept the night Ronald Reagan, "the fascist gun in the West," sent the Pigs into Berkeley. Not everyone wept though. Three thousand miles away in the part of the NATION called the Lower East Side, someone tried to fire-bomb the Fillmore in retaliation. They missed and burned down the building next door. Too bad in a way cause most of us used to rip off the Lion Supermarket there when we had to eat and had no dough. Fans poured out into the streets even though The Who (who else) kept playin away. They were so zonked into their thing that Peter Townshend kicked a plainclothes cop in the balls when he tried to make an announcement and got arrested. I think it might be helpful if you know about this stuff before you judge the WOODSTOCK NATION. It didn't just happen in those three days, it was a long time comin. This is something else you should know:

> Stamford, Connecticut: Today the publisher of *Reader's Digest* was stabbed by his sixteen-year-old son. He had just returned from a businessman's luncheon in which he delivered what was termed an "anti-hippie" speech. 21

½ **of Elvis Presley**

People of all shapes and sizes are always coming up to me and asking me why I do what I do or am what I am. As I explained in the first book I can lay a hundred explanations all at once on em or just drop the Bomb. The Bomb meaning that one punch line. That put-on that turns everything you just said upside down. Like dig this, for example. The first book has a paragraph missing at the end. Can you imagine that? The publishers cut out the punch line because it would mean using a whole new page. Anyway, here it is:

> "Well, I guess I'm getting a little tired so I think
> I'll buzz over to the Gem Spa for an egg cream
> and end it. See you after the Revolution when,
> of course, it'll be business as usual.

See, it's the "humbler" when you really let people know you're only in it for kicks and stuff and it keeps them off that follower-nagging-trip that makes you feel like a martyr, and an itchy martyr at that! It keeps down the "Dear Abbie" mail.

So when people ask a lead-in question like that, they are kind of open for a Zen jab that might help them see that they're really just like me and me like them, the only difference being that I love my work. Often when they ask those questions they ask, "How come you're a radical?" or "How come a hippie?" or "How can you say things like 'Kids should kill their parents?' " I make up a lot of stories, but now for the first time I'm about to tell the TRUTH, the whole TRUTH and nothing but the TRUTH.

Back during the 1950's me and the guys I bummed around with when I got thrown out of school wore

pegged pants, had DA haircuts, blue suede shoes, and hung around pool halls swearing and spitting a lot. The music we listened to was called race-records and then rhythm and blues. Varetta Dillard singing "Mercy Mister Percy" was the first race-record I ever heard. We dug stuff like Earl Bostic, James Moody, the Midnighters, Joe Turner, and later the Drifters and Fats Domino. It was all 45 rpm stuff which made for easy swipin, simple under-the-jacket stuff. The trouble was that very few stores carried the stuff cause Patti Page singing about porcelain "Old Cape Cod" and Frankie Laine moaning "I Believe" religious hymns and Tony Bennett singing funky Tony Bennett Blues was all the stores knew. On the radio too there was just Symphony Sid out of Boston and later Moondog out of New York. We were two hundred and fifty miles from New York and had to rig up a roof antenna to hear ol Alan Freed bang a telephone book on the table while he spun out the Sound. The

Sound was SAXOPHONE and it was "Unh — unh — stick — it — in — wa — doo — was." Dances were all grunts and belts with names like the Ginny-Crawl and Roxbury Mule, and there were very few of us doing it. You just didn't do the Dirty Boogie to Theresa Brewer, no sir, and not at the Totem Pole in Newton, Mass., no man, definitely not. The whole scene except for a few of us hoods — I think that's what we preferred to be called especially if we had read *A Stone for Danny Fisher* and *The Amboy Dukes* — so except for us hoods and Bill Haley and his Comets, the whole fuckin scene was Black. Black-Ass sockin it out and humpin a sax while sweat poured out in buckets. "Shake, baby, shake, baby, shake, till the meat rolls off your bones" and "I'm gonna roll like a big wheel through the Georgia cotton fields, Honey Hush" — God that music sure gave you a boner and gettin laid then wasn't like it is today so you'd slick your hair with grease and learn how to pick your

teeth with a toothpick instead.

Then it happened. It was the first taste I got of the Culture-Vultures. I didn't know the term then, in fact I knew shit about any kind of politics, except whether or not you were gonna pay up if you lost the game of nine ball like you said you would. "I didn't know nothin" (to coin a popular phrase of the time). But somehow I smelled a fish. "Sh-boom, Sh-boom, eya-ta-ta-ta-ta-ta-ta, Sh-boom Sh-boom, if I could take you home again, Sh-boom, Sh-boom..." All of a sudden you heard it not being sung by the Chords, but by a strange group that didn't sing it from the guts out. They sang it obscene, fake, commercial, phony. I don't know what it was, but the group, they were clean as all hell, whiter than Ivory Snow and Grace Kelly and they were called the CREWCUTS. Motherfuckin WASPS. We were soon to learn there was a whole fuckin pack of WASPS buzzin around and they were all related to that bitch Patti Page and worse, Ezio Pinza and Mary Martin. Their leader was a lean corn flake named Pat Boone who ran around ripping off black-ass rock-and-roll and dressin it up with white bucks! WHITE BUCKS! Stepping on punks' white bucks as they came home from school was in fact among my first political acts, but even this didn't repay the feeling of wretched puke you felt when you pictured Snookie Lanson singing "Earth Angel" on the Lucky Strike Hit Parade.

Nothing else more than that rip-off of black music made me more ashamed of being white than anything, not even the "woman who came in on Thursdays." But all of a sudden, some dude came struttin up from down in the South somewhere. He dug bikes like in "The Wild One" and he smirked like James Dean in everything. He was a tough-ass motherfucker and he sang from the inside out and yet he was white. He belted it out and what he said was get the fuck off my blue suede shoes, get your fuckin crew-cut, white-buck, sissy boots off my blues. Get your big dynaflo Buick off the fuckin road and let my chopped and channeled '49 Merc fly. Get those fuckin tweeds out of Ware Pratt's and let me see those sweet talkin pegs. And baby, you better move quick or you won't just be cryin in the chapel, you'll be dyin.

Then event two happened in the life of said Communist-Bastard. Ed Sullivan, you know Ed Sullivan, well, he owned the whole plantation in those days. If you weren't on the Sullivan Shooow you didn't exist. Ed Sullivan, the Rock of Ages, who two months ago said when introducing James Earl Jones, "Ladies and gentlemen, a credit to anybody's race." Now Big Ed after much hassle had agreed to put Elvis on live. Wow! Elvis was gonna do "Heartbreak Hotel" and "Blue Suede Shoes" and all the gang came over to watch. It was Sunday night about 8:30 p.m. sometime in the late fifties.

You know what? We never did get to see his blue suedes, in fact the truth of it is, we never got to see anything below Elvis' navel! It was only the bottom half of Elvis that mattered, and fucking Ed Sullivan and CBS-TV and Madison Avenue and FCC and the Pentagon could never understand that. I got a little dizzy watching the top half of Elvis bobbin around like a fishin cork in a bathtub and staggered into the john, pukin up all the booze and Devil Dogs and with it a lot more. "Hey man, you O.K.?" asked my buddy, Hack. "Yeh, sure, how the hell can they do that? If I see that Sullivan I'm gonna push his fuckin face in."

Give the People What They Want

I'm finally glad I got a chance to tell that story. I like it better than the one about being radicalized by HUAC in San Francisco or Bull Connor in Birmingham. I like it better because it lets me talk to the folks who live in WOODSTOCK NATION. It helps to get the message out. Back then Elvis spoke the words of POWER TO THE PEOPLE, to the fringe ones, the visitors that came to taste of freedom. You organize around arrests and harassment for in the end there is really not that much difference between repression and oppression, only in the minds of SDS theoreticians. Dig it, Mark Rudd is facing fifteen years on a drug bust and I talk about it more than he does! It's just not relevant to his DOME WORLD of politics. I just want to tell a little story that I heard and if you see Mark around pass it on to him. He doesn't like the title of my books so he doesn't read them.

Once upon a time some maggots started a revolution. It was about 1917 I think and there were these maggots in all the food on this ship. The men were pissed-off as all hell but they had no idea what the fuck to do. They didn't know from reformism and from imperialism and revisionism and any of that shit. All they knew was maggots. Now along comes some sneaky fucks who were definitely outside agitators and didn't really give a shit about maggots. Somehow their instincts told them that from maggots you could point to the captain of the ship and then to the Czar of Russia and maybe even later *Potemkin* might make a groovy movie so they dropped a few hints and soon, very soon, there was a mighty mutiny and well the rest is all distorted in the history books. SDS would have shouted "maggots are reformist" and called the sailors irrelevant or petit bourgeois, or lumpenproletariat, or outside the Third World, or white, hence unreachable. Unreachable because they were worthless. Worthless! That's it! The reason SDS couldn't relate to the WOODSTOCK NATION was because they saw the people as worthless which of course means they see themselves as worthless which is mighty weird and no fun at all. So if you see Mark and the others comin out your way, tell em we're still friends even though the left sucks. They'll understand it cause deep down they're hippies just like us.

DAISY JOHNSON GO TO THE RED TENT IN THE HOG FARM. MYRON COHEN WANTS TO MARRY YOU.

An army without culture is a dull-witted army, and a dull-witted army cannot defeat the enemy.

> Mao Tse-Tung, "The United Front in Cultural Work" (October 30, 1944), Selected Works, Vol. III, p. 235.

MARY BE SURE TO CALL YOUR MOTHER

What we demand is the unity of politics and art, the unity of content and form, the unity of revolutionary political content and the highest possible perfection of artistic form. Works of art which lack artistic quality have no force, however progressive they are politically.

> Talks at the Yenan Forum on Literature and Art (May, 1942) *Selected Works,* Vol. III, p. 84.

IMPORTANT: SUPER JOEL GET IN TOUCH WITH THE CONSPIRACY OFFICE

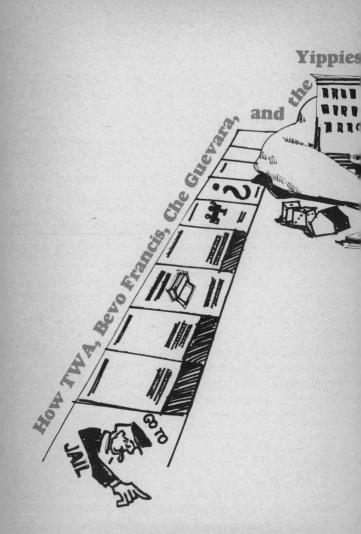

Yippies

and the

How TWA, Bevo Francis, Che Guevara,

GO TO JAIL

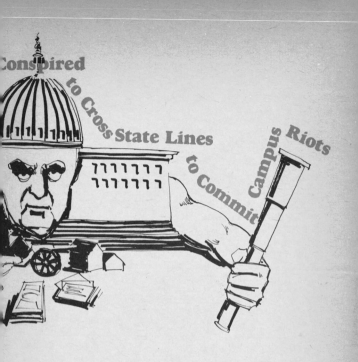

Conspired to Cross State Lines to Commit Campus Riots

Up in the sky fellow conspirators! What would we do without airplanes? Sterile lobbies, tunnel sleeves, steel Howard Johnson bellies of great birds. So natural for us, our horizontal elevators, as McLuhan would say. I wondered where Bruce and J.D. were, two FBI agents that usually accompany me with a tape recorder — Mechanical Boswells recording that great Conspiracy in the Sky. They would have dug the plane ride out of Buffalo after the hugest Dope Conference in history. See, I have this thing about not fastening my seat belt. It's against my religion to tie myself up. Anyway I was so high from Free Buffalo that even if the plane went down I'd keep on flyin. Well, usually stewardesses won't do much after I explain that I will not hold them responsible for my death. That is if they don't ball me and stuff like that. This one was a 31 real bitch though, and it's early Sunday morning hang-over time and she says, "We have radioed ahead to the FBI who are going to arrest you for not obeying Federal Aviation Code 27-2B" something or other. Well, she was only half bluffin cause it was only local Rochester cops.

But that's ancient history and now we were headed for Antioch. Antioch in Asia Minor where Paul got mobbed out of town for provocative gestures like crossing himself. Nah, I'm only kiddin — this Antioch is Hippie Haven. It's our version of R & R (rest and recreation for you who weren't in the army). Each time we flew over another state line I thought of the Attorney General standing on the Justice Department roof with a giant telescope keeping count and playing Monopoly. "Go directly to jail. Do not pass Pennsylvania. Do not collect $200 from the Student Union." I was exhausted. Four of us potential conspirators met all night before leaving to cross state lines again. We were trying to puzzle out the Chicago mess. We were to be indicted on March 11th by the Federal Grand Jury, and on March 10th the Supreme Court socked in a decision on wire-tapping which, on the surface, appeared to fuck the Justice Department right up the ass. Seems we had a right to see the transcripts of all those secret coded telephone calls we make.

Well, PIG NATION says it doesn't want to admit that it is bugging a certain foreign embassy that we call from time to time to check on the sugar crop. It's weird because it's admitting it right on the front page of *The New York Times!* Nobody understood what

32   the Supreme Court decision meant but everyone

thought without the wire-tapping evidence we'd beat the conspiracy indictments about to come out of Chicago.

Attorney General Mitchell must really have been pissed. He had been on every TV set yakkin about professional agitators crossing state lines to get their college degrees, and if it wasn't the conspiracy rap for Chicago, he'd soon get something else on us.

If the phone was bugged and the government was afraid to have it come out in court maybe we had immunity from all Federal laws? I made a note to call my lawyer and get a list of every Federal law and another note to return by way of Washington to ask Edward Bennett Williams, who argued the case, "What the fuck is going on?" Not that I really cared; spring was coming and it had been a rotten yellow winter filled with hepatitis the Government injected in me during captivity in the D.C. jail.

I checked my bag — one Yippie film, ten copies of *Fuck the System;* Mao's little red book; recipes for Molotov cocktails, electric Koolaid and digger stew; a children's game manufactured in Albania called "Kick the Yankees in the Balls"; five hundred YIPPIE! buttons and ten million dollars worth of pot which I was furiously trying to smoke up before we were commanded to move into an upright position, seeing as how I can't get vertically stoned.

Eric, Yippie Agent in charge of Ohio, was smiling in the airport lobby. I coughed all the way to Antioch explaining that my lungs were not accustomed to fresh air. It didn't take long to figure out where Antioch's head was at. There are lots of progressive nursery schools, but there the kiddies are so big!

Most issues that are being fought for at other schools were won at Antioch ten years ago. Perhaps won is not the right word, they were liberally given. Like the big sheet of paper over the men's pissing stall for grafitti. But, well Antioch would be the dream school for most students given what they now have. No ROTC, close teacher-student community relations, people turn on and fuck everywhere, naked swim-ins in the gym pool, a black dorm, nice woods, co-ed dorms, Sunday tourists who drive through to stare at the commie-hippies, and so much love and identity-searching. It was all "Who am I?" stuff. Everything was so beautiful, I was completely bored after three hours. The school lacked the energy that comes from struggle. When I was leaving the next day Eric remarked, "You know surveys show that 55 per cent of us end up in large corporations." What "Hair" is to Broadway, Antioch is to the universities. That's not really a put-down. If you can't fuck you might as well jerk off. Antioch is the best play going, that is, if you've got about $25,000 for an orchestra seat.

Next stop was Wright State, owned by the National Cash Register Company. I rapped to a group on the grass doing my little jive-ass sales pitch when a big "NO SALE" flashed on the Science Building and I decided to split. I was already preparing for the night show; I didn't want to waste the juice. A battle was brewing and I was aching for a fight.

We were headed for Rio (Rye-O) Grande College and two kids, one the school's only hippy, had driven three hours to Antioch to get me to come. Seems their favorite teacher was getting bounced for "immaturity." There had never been a demonstration there, demonstrations are forbidden. The school is so bad it doesn't even have accreditation. Its only claim to fame is a 7-foot basketball player named Bevo Francis who fifteen years ago got them in *Life* magazine when he scored a hundred points in a game against Pygmy U. Bevo was in high school when he played for Rio Grande, no one knows whether he actually graduated from Rio Grande, but they're namin a dorm after him anyway. He used to run around the country like some Mountain of White Blubber while the Harlem Globe Trotters ran circles around him. Some say Bevo is now running the State Department but the truth is the sorry big fella is driving a dump truck in Pennsylvania.

Rio Grande College is in Rio Grande, Ohio (population: 300), ten miles west of West Virginia. The barber is the mayor. There is one cop in town. He got the job for winning a pheasant hunt. I was invited by the most radical group on campus (the Young Democrats) which had been formed the day before. As we bounced along through the empty cornfields in the old Ford the troublemakers filled me in on all the shit. The Klan had promised a cross-burning. The jocks were pissed and capable of trouble. They had just hung a cat to celebrate my coming and dropped lighted cherry bombs inside some dogs. Alphus Christiansen, President and Supreme Ruler, had left unexpectedly for parts unknown when he heard the news. The teacher, Bill Christopher, a nice gentle guy, was being thrown out for three reasons.

1. Writing a letter to the campus newspaper criticizing local cultural apathy and recommending an Appalachia studies program.

2. Eating cupcakes at a faculty meeting.

3. Using profanity in front of another teacher (the exact word was "bitch").

I had trouble believing all this! I mean with all the shit flying around colleges and high schools these days. I wondered if Rio Grande, or Postdam U. or New Paltz, or Richmond or any of the fifty or so small schools I visited were important to Mitchell and NATIONAL SECURITY? I wondered if Mitchell had his telescope on Rio Grande? He might though, cause there is an amazing article in the April, 1969 *True* magazine about how PIG NATION nailed Che. They have developed aerial reconnaissance planes that at fifteen hundred feet can takes pictures of a guy and tell how long it's been since he shaved. I wonder how Che would have responded to the news that you

35

couldn't eat cupcakes at Rio Grande? I love you Che ... Che ... Che ... Che ...

My head filled with images of machine-gunning Batista as we passed a pig farm. It's very poor land out there. A special kind of poverty different from Mississippi and the Lower East Side. I had never seen that kind before -- well, yeah, in Boone, Kentucky -- but that was a good time ago and I wasn't really looking. Seems there is coal under the ground there and around the early 1900's the mine owners signed contracts with the farmers allowing them the right to get the coal out of the ground by "any means necessary." In those days it worked O.K. Shit! What's a little hole here and there? But then came huge Trucks and Steam Shovels and Bulldozers. The Capitalist Pigs chewed up all the hills. They dug up the crops just to get at the coal. The farmers fought back but got fucked by the courts. In the end they were forced to lease out their land to the mining syndicates and go to work in the mines, still paying taxes on their own land. Each year they went deeper in debt. With each new debt came another kid and tuberculosis and hookworm and that Ben Shahn 1930's look of hunger. It is the saddest poverty in the nation The kind you used to cry about when Pete Seeger sang Union songs.

When we arrived I met Bill Christopher and asked him what the fuck he wanted to stay here for. He said, "I think I have something to teach the kids." Shit! It was all gettin so country honest. I was feeling a bit hardened by long complicated discussions at Antioch about confrontational politics, cybernetic revolution and real high-falutin theoretical bullshit. It was good to be with real people again. Bill showed me the faculty handbook with such gems as "nothing controversial that is not related to the subject matter shall be discussed in class."

The recreation hall was packed when we walked in. It was a clankety old wooden building that I immediately loved, having just spoken in about a hundred ultramodern paneled, soft-lighted mechanical mind-trap designed to rot your brain. The guys I was with, Steve Troyanovich and Jeff Gleiss, were shaking with ecstasy. Everybody had come out, even the mayor. It was as if Bevo was back in town! They didn't believe their eyes but there were ball players, black students (ten of them)... hillbillies, hippies (one), straights, ex-marines, teachers, six or seven hundred out of a one thousand student body. A teacher who had been thrown out last year even come back. They had never seen a conspiring yippie-hippie-communist-drugged-sex-maniac, never mind one who had done all that in Chicago and gone to Russia for instructions and punched the head of HUAC and was taking LSD and they say he's gonna show obscene movies! "This we gotta see!" And they settled back in their seats ready for the show. I turned down an introduction (which I always do), jumped up on the stage and announced, "This is a fuckin movie about Pigs and Yippies. If you're stoned real good you can see the people fuckin in the grass. It cost me and my friends twelve bucks to make it and it ain't won no awards." Lights out, "Here's Yippie." Bang! Mayor Daley appears. There is applause but wait — here come the Yippies pouring through the gates of the city jumping to Phil Ochs and "I Ain't Marching Anymore." The crowd was yelling for the Freaks. By the end of the film, everybody was jumpin up and down, hissing the cops, laughing their asses off. There ain't nothing SDS got that coulda worked that night at Rio Grande but that raggedy-ass movie did it. I jumped up at the end. They were all cheering like it was a basketball game. "I'm Huey Newton and I'm here to burn down the school!" It's a wild-ass rap, throwing away the mike, ripping off my shirt, yelling about how we are getting stepped on. "This is General Motors and you are the cars. Does General Motors ask the cars if they want all that fuckin chrome?" Dig it! Fun and sadness and sittin on the edge of the stage, cryin about how we are gettin gassed and beaten and arrested. Somebody held up the sissy V sign and I yelled, "Fuck that! We are at war!" I challenged the Klan, calling them chicken-shit.

It's sweet talking about cupcakes and freedom and new ways of living the FUTURE. Because WE ARE THE FUTURE! It was the best since in Lincoln Park and I was happy cause I knew the winter was over. It ended on a down-beat suspenseful-like-hanging-slow-in-the-air, "The freak show is over ...what are you going to do??? Hum???" I mumbled as I walked down the steps of the stage and up and down the rows of stunned students..."What you going to do now, hum? Why don't somebody else get up there and say what is on his mind!...no commies in this school?...No agitators?...No cat hangers? ... SI-LENCE ...then one kid stuttered up to the front and the place went wild. "I'm gonna take a few books out of the library tomorrow and sit out on the steps and read em and if they don't let Mr. Christopher stay.. (gulp)...I might just not bring em back." Yippie! Then another and another got up. A jock even. A hillbilly drawled out one of the most beautiful raps I ever heard. A teacher gave an old-fashioned rap about what education means; then a kid got up and chal-lenged one of the members of the Administration who was sitting in the audience to answer the com-plaints. Everyone was screamin and stompin but he didn't say a word. A black cat got up on the stage. A chubby guy with his shirt hanging out ... "I'm one of those drunken niggers you see around here every once in a while ... you gotta be drunk to go to this school ..." Everybody's hootin and yellin. Another black got up, an athlete, "I'm goin out to the library and take some books out too ... I gotta two-thousand-dollar-a-year scholarship at stake but they can shove it if I can't have my dignity." And then the call for com-mitment. "How many comin out tomorrow?" and four hundred Freemen jumped up with their fists in the air. Steve and Jeff were ballin and I must admit I ain't felt that good for quite a while either and I was ballin too.

We talked most of the night in some pad and started

out at 6:00 a.m. – two hours to the airport.

On the way little kids in their yellow submarine bus were going to school. They spotted my long hair and started all crowdin up to the windows. They got one open and a skinny arm juts out with two fingers making the sign of the V and we were all laughin and waving to the kids. "I wonder if we got some time to visit their school," I said, "they might dig that Yippie film..." "Aw, come on," Steve said, "leave some stuff for us. This conspiracy is good smokin shit."

So I got up on the plane, me and all the other executives, and I sang em "Who made the mine owners, sing the proud bells of Dum-dum" and counted the state lines as we hummed back East. "1 Boundary--2 Boundary--3 Boundary," John Mitchell, we just dig to play Monopoly, wait until we get to Park Place!

Postscript

Attorney General Mitchell decided to knock over the Monopoly board and indict eight of us for Conspiracy, wire-tapping or no wire-tapping ruling. Fuck the Supreme Court! Nixon was at war with them anyhow – the decision to continue wire-tapping along with the Anti-riot Act under which we were being charged, gave Nixon plenty of good muscle to put down the campus revolts. Ten years for wanting to have a festival in a public park even if the city refused us a permit! I wonder if he or Boss Daley had read the following decision:

Wheresoever the title of streets and parks may rest, they have immemorially been held in trust for the use of the public and, time out of mind, have been used for the purposes of assembly for communicating thoughts between citizens and discussing public questions. Such use of the streets and public places has, from ancient times, been part of the privileges, immunities, rights, and liberties of citizens.

Shuttles vs. Alabama 37 *Law Week*
4203, p. 4204 (1969) Decision
Supreme Court, Justice Stewart
Potter speaking.   39

I wonder if Mitchell wiped his ass with *Law Week* the way Lenny Bruce used to do. I wonder if he had ever even heard of Lenny Bruce. Oh well, I suppose you're wondering whatever happened to Rio Grande? The next day, eighty-one kids got booted out of school and more got arrested when they failed to produce ID cards while standing around in front of the library arguing about what to do next. They ain't leavin the area though and they think they got something good goin not only at the college but in the high school as well where the real action is happening. Dig it PIG NATION; if you're feeling down on campus revolts wait until you see the high schools this year. God it's gonna be a swingin year as we fly into the seventies. I'm making a note to speak at my grammar school, where ol lady Brigham used to drill us over and over again on how to make Ovals and Sitstraightintheseat. Hell, no wonder we were all crazy! You ever try doing Ovals all day. Nothin but round fuckin Ovals except for the time you had to practice SILENCE by sitting with your ass against the back of the chair, two feet squarely on the floor and hands clasped in prayer style ...... Praying for recess to come.

Moonshine

Dear Earth and especially that section of it referred to as "outside the free world":

Last night a group of us weirdos sat up all night and watched what has to be the greatest TV show, in fact, the "Greatest Show on Earth," as old John Ringling North of circus fame would have put it. "Armstrong slithers out of the capsule..." One really can't help but get caught up in the majesty of it all, the holiness, this birth of the New Age. There they are now. Wow! Is it real? Or is it one of those back-lot Hollywood sets...it's too bad Walt Disney didn't live to see this one...Yep! It's beyond 2001! Stanley Kubrick's gotta be head of NASA...did some weird gremlin decide just one week before the moon-shot to play Dr.

Strangelove on the Late Show? Look at em jumping around. When they leap it's poetry, when they talk, even some number-jumbo, you're aware that in one hundred years, one thousand years, this will endure as an art form.

One tries not to be cynical; after all, they are jumping around on the fuckin moon and no matter what you think of PIG NATION, you have to admit that it does have a good special effects department. Whee! Look at em bounce around. What is he gonna do? Will he piss on the moon? Will he say, "Send up some booze and broads, we don't want to go back?" Nah, no bits ... well, what do you expect? This albino crewcut has been selected with more precision than the American Machine selects a president. Man, this cat is the un-known soldier from Arlington Cemetery, resurrected just for this special mission. A number-one-all-Amerikan cracker. I mean did you dig his parents. Mr. and Mrs. A-OK Armstrong — the Mom and Pop of Moonman ... Moonman, the all-time comic strip hero. No, this ain't a comic strip. It's a radio show from the late forties, that's it! "Wheaties the all-American Breakfast Cereal brings you Jack Armstrong the All-American Boy." No shit! Do you believe that! Now ladies and gentlemen, "This hour of the Voyage to the Moon is brought to you by Kelloggs ... A small step (snap), for man (crackle), a giant step for mankind (pop)." The Ruskies, they have the technological capacity to get to the moon, that is if the country felt like sinking 34 billion into being first. They might have pulled it off, but not them, not anyone but good ol PIG NATION with a used-car dealer for president, could have thought about selling time to sponsors to broadcast the flight of Apollo 11. I mean, isn't that the sort of PIG ART that has come to make Amerika great? Can you really picture even Western Imperialist Columbus off to conquer the New World with a sign on the side of his ship that says, "Eat Genoa Salami." Only in Amerika.

PIG NATION's brain is its special effects department　　41

and its heart is an ad agency. Its statesmanship is lodged someplace in its asshole.

I mean, who among us is ready to follow Spiro Agnew, torch in hand, into the Aquarian Age. "Our peace council will present plans to land a MAN on MARS by the year two thousand." My God what a genius, what daring, what imagination. There you go world. Fuck you Mao. Fuck you Galileo. Fuck you Darwin. Dig PIG NATION's genius — Spiro T. Agnew. We take you now to the year two thousand A.D. ladies and gentlemen:

"Here comes the moment we've all been waiting for. Captain Amerika is about to shake hands with ZQRTS, Martian Leader and delegate to the Intergalactic Union. It is all coming true just like the prophetic wisdom of the Amerikan genius Vice President Agnew predicted when he launched mankind on its greatest adventure ever. Captain Amerika is to present ZQRTS with an Amerikan flag and a year's supply of MARS BARS." (Would you believe Milky Ways?)

The only thing wrong with the whole trip was that Amerika brought its morality with it when, like some senile dinosaur, it slid out of the capsule 250,000 miles away and stepped its virgin boot into the sea of moondust. It's really sad. The flag bit, I mean. What Pig in the Pentagon ordered the project that would fix the flag so it would fly forever unfurled like some perpetual hard-on in space? I mean why must the flag be unfurled or is this just another Kodak Scenic Wonder Sight where tourists can stop and send photos home to the relatives, "Having a wonderful time, wish you were here."

And now Pig Leader Nixon would like a chance to sell the world this flashy two-seater space module step right up folks, get in line. And the TV screen splits in two and a little color cartoon figure in red yellow and blue, with a head that has been mashed in by a vise appears in the top left corner. In a squeaky voice comes, "My fellow earthmen..."

I can't take it...I walk out on the roof. I just got to be alone. It's a foggy night, the Con Edison plant across the street is pouring the wastes we in New York have come to love, into the sky. It's impossible to see the Empire State Building, another Amerikan monument, even though it's only twenty blocks away, all lit up too, and besides as we all know, the biggest fuckin thing around. All the shit in the air (excuse me, "wastes" — isn't that what they call it when astronauts shit—"Making waste on the moon"?) pours out of these three huge funnels, but what the fuck, the funnels are painted red, white and blue just like that flag up there...

So world, and especially that section that Walter Cronkite refers to as "outside the free world," to you Niggers of the world, I would like to take a moment aside from the hectic nature of our revolution, designed to wipe out the disease of competitive capitalism, and apologize for this alien country in which we find ourselves. Furthermore, I would like to let you know that young people here in WOODSTOCK NATION are learning to fly in space...some day we too will fly off in some communal capsule, Blacks, Puerto Ricans, Hippies, liberated women, young workers on the line, and G.I.'s sitting in stockades because they don't want to go to Vietnam. There will be a whole mess of us laughing and getting stoned on our way to OUTERSPACE, and the first thing, the very first thing we're gonna do out there is to rip down that fuckin flag on the moon.

Power to the People,
Abbie Earthman
Woodstock Nation

43

Che's Last Letter

to the youth of the United States

I write to you huddled in blankets.
Damp, shivering, cold, temporarily dejected
over recent military set backs. We are
somewhere in the jungles of Bolivia
surrounded by the enemy, cut off from
all supplies. Struggling against
immense odds. My thoughts turn to the
young people struggling for a chance at
life in the bowels of plastic America
cut off from the lifeline of human
existance. For you, like us, we are also
surrounded. I recall the time I worked
as a waiter in Miami Beach hotel
and my frequent visits to New York and
know that people in the second half of
the twentieth century are not destined
to play out their lives in either the
jungles of Bolivia or Manhattan. Surely
the destiny of man was to lift
himself out of the jungle. Out of an
economic system that forced him to
behave like a beast of prey. Out of a
corresponding socio-religious system
that cherished money and greed and

hatred and inhumanity. I know you will say, "We know all that but what do you offer? More killing? A subtle change in things? What is so revolutionary about your revolution?" But of course you are cynical. Your universities teach you to be eternal cynics, a cynicism that can be only drowned in alcohol and diet pills and psychoanalysts and golf. Forget your cynicism. There is no one who has more respect for life than a revolutionist. I am by profession a doctor. I found, however, to heal bodies under an inhuman system, such as existed then and now in my native Argentina was corrupt. So I left to join Fidel and the others and help in my small way to build the revolution in Cuba. What we did was to establish a model to show that under great oppressive odds radical social change can take place. You must shed the bandages bound around your eyes by the press in your country. You must go to Cuba and experience what has happened there over the past ten years.

Even as we realized victory in Cuba, we knew that the battle had just begun. For a revolution, in order to be a true revolution, must be a world revolution. To achieve that world revolution, you the children of the Yankees must lend a hand. You must vomit forth your cynicism in the streets of your cities. You must mount an unrelenting attack on everything the bastards that rule your country hold dear. You must refuse to serve in their armies, you must reject the heroin offered in their universities, you must become clogs in their productive machinery. Your struggle will be a long and arduous one. It will not come easy. There are no guide rules to apply to revolution. Each country is unique and your struggle is the most unique of all, for your repression is of a very peculiar nature. Search for brothers and sisters in the struggle. Steel yourself inside for the oppressive blows that will greet each new victory. Learn patience. Learn how to survive. It will not be all hardship and suffering as others have warned. What is suffering comrades? Even as I write knowing death is coming over that hill not five hundreds yards away I would not go back to bring a respected professional in a system I detested. That is the true death of the spirit. No, although my health is failing, physical death is approaching and our plans here have met with disaster, I know we have won. Not for ourselves but for those who will follow us into these jungles of reality and into the jungles of their own minds to strike that blow for freedom. Men of revolutionary vision and action are sprouting everywhere. Like wild flowers bursting the overpowering prison of cement roads they grow Vietnam, Angola, Guatemala, Paris and now even in the heart of the Steel Goliath. Little Davids strike hard and deep. Vinceremos.

Che

This was part of a little plot Jerry Rubin, Ed Sanders and I worked up, with plans to "discover the letters in the Bolivian jungles" and sell them to *Ramparts*. We blew it though and they ended up in *The Realist* for free.

Fuck the Flag

Last summer, just a few days before Congress zipped through the law making it illegal to conspire to run a Pig for president in the streets of Chicago, they passed a federal law protecting the flag from "deface-ment and defiling." The maximum penalty is one year in jail and a $1000 fine. (The only other country to have just passed a similar law is Russia.) The flag was not the only national symbol to be protected. Previous laws gave protection to Smoky the Bear, the 4-H Club's cloverleaf, and the Swiss flag (?). For example, anyone who "defaces a facsimile of Smoky the Bear is subject to a $250 fine and six months in jail."*

*Volume 18, U.S. Code Sections 700 and 711.

My arrest (for wearing a flag shirt) at the HUAC hearing last October was the first arrest under the federal law. At the trial I was found guilty and given a thirty-day sentence which is just coming up for appeal. A transcript of the trial can be found in the November, 1968 issue of *The Realist*. That the law is so vague that it would make Uncle Sam, drum majorettes and candidates who sport red, white and blue hats and ties criminals is relatively unimportant to the federal government. They have adopted Catch-22 as their motto which states, if you remember, "we can put anybody in jail who we don't like no matter what the fuck the constitution says."

Since my conviction there have been numerous others. Edward Franz, a freshman at Virginia Commonwealth University, was sentenced to a year in jail for wearing a flag vest. Wearing the same style vest, a sixteen-year-old Boston guy visiting Alexandria, Virginia, was arrested and "banished from the city of Alexandria until the age of 21." Dig that sentence! A student at Franklin Marshall College in Lancaster was recently busted for using the flag as a bedspread, and on and on, across the country, with about thirty such cases in the past few months. Of course not everyone who wears a flag shirt or dress gets arrested, just as not everyone who smokes pot goes to jail. The flag design is a current mod-fashion among the rich. Ads for dresses and vests appeared recently in *The New York Times*, *Los Angeles Times* and the *San Francisco Examiner*, to name a few. Phyllis Diller has appeared on TV in a flag mini-skirt and companies are doing a brisk business in flag lighters (for draft cards?) flag chairs, flag ties, flag hats, flag banks, flag dishes, flag pencil holders, and there is a rumor that a flag diaphragm is on the way.

Perhaps a clue as to why the government is so anxious to prosecute us undesirables is found in a brief filed in the District of Columbia Court of Appeals by

Department of Justice Attorney Mervyn Hamburg to

...ort the law and their case against me. The ...ance of a flag in developing a sense of loyalty t... ...onal entity has been the subject of numer... ...ys." The first essay the U.S. Government quo... ...e following:

...itler, *Mein Kampf,* translated by Manheim ...(Houghton Mifflin, 1943), p. 492:

...he organization of our monitor troop clarified ...a very important question. Up till then the ...movement possessed no party insignia and no ...party flag. The absence of such symbols no... ...only had momentary disadvantages, but was ...intolerable for the future. The disadvantages ...consisted above all in the fact that the party ...comrades lacked an outward sign of their ...common bond, while it was unbearable for the ...future to dispense with a sign which possessed ...the character of a symbol of the movement and ...could as such be opposed to the International ...What importance must be attributed to such a ...symbol from the psychological point of view ... ...had even in my youth more than one occasion ...to recognize and also emotionally to under... ...stand. Then, after the War, I experienced a mass ...demonstration of the Marxists in front of the ...Royal Palace and the Lustgarten. A sea of red ...flags, red scarves, and red flowers gave to this ...demonstration, in which an estimated hundred ...and twenty thousand persons took part, an ...aspect that was gigantic from the purely ex... ...ternal point of view. I myself could feel and ...understand how easily the man of the people ...succumbs to the suggestive magic of a spectacle ...so grandiose in effect.

...always knew that Hitler was running the S... ...partment, now it seems he has taken over ...tice Department as well?"*

...cently the District Court of Appeals upheld the const... ...ality of this law and the case is now in the proces... ...appealed to the Supreme Court.

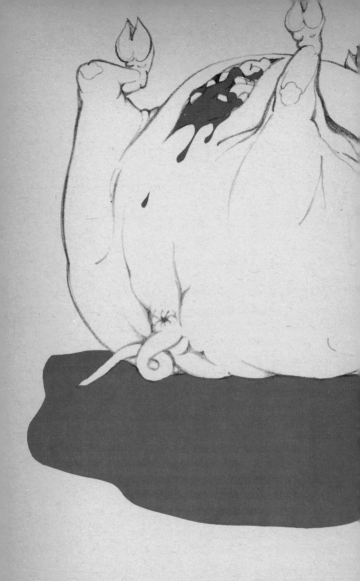

Death to the Pigs Who Invade O

It's July fifteenth,* 2 a.m. on a farm somewhere in Ann Arbor, Michigan. It's a beautiful warm night, filled with a starry blue sky waiting for the astronauts to violate its silence. Lying on your back you can look up and repeat all the old hippy cliches to yourself about dropping out and heading for the country. Why not? After all, on a clear night in New York City up on my roof I can sometimes see two stars and Anita jokes about how they must be attached to a long electric wire that comes out of the Con Ed

ds

*Not really — It's August 23rd and I'm writing upside down on the floor.

building across the street, for there are no clear nights in New York. There is an underground newspaper conference going on at the farm. It's a good place to start describing some of the changes that have gone down in the hip community over the past few years. For the underground press is the molder and chronicler of the amorphous body of long-haired young freaks you see sticking their tongue out at you in the TV news at night or luring your daughter to a rock-and-roll dance in the park.

NIXON DECLARES WAR ON DRUGS

PEOPLE LIBERATE PARK

STREET FIGHTING IN MADISON ENTERS
    SECOND DAY

10,000 CRASH GATES AT MUSIC FESTIVAL

It has been an awkward time of anxieties and doubts. I mean like what the fuck was I doing? On April ninth, I stood before a seventy-four-year-old bald-headed judge* and heard him read this mumbo jumbo, 1984 indictment and I couldn't help but feel a bit silly standing there with my hair climbing down the back of the blue Chicago policeman's shirt I was wearing. Conspiracy! Wow!

Were we freaks really a threat? I had just come from the SDS convention in Chicago. It was weird. People throwing red books at each other is a strange form of revolution?? Throughout the conference, I marveled at how little I understood what was being said. Songs like "male chauvinism" "petit bourgeois revisionist," "puppet lackeys," "tool of the military-industrial complex," and "member of the proletariat vanguard waging the relentless battle against imperialism" were sung and other tunes that escape me for the moment. They are vibrations in another plastic dome. Going to that SDS conference was a bummer. I mean when fifty guys jumped up at some point, as if the speaker

---

*Judge Julius Hoffman not only is determined to send us up the river for ten years, but he is also spreading the vicious lie that I'm his illegitimate son. The Judge has tired blood. Why not send him some Geritol?

at the rostrum has landed with a good left hook, and, holding up red books, shouted, "Mao! Mao! Mao Tse-Tung!" you would think this would be O.K., but no, not if the group was Revolutionary Youth Movement Number Two. So not to let them slip by their left vanguard, up pops Progressive Labor Party in the balcony and shouts in unison, "Beware those who wave the red flag to oppose the red flag." You can see why I was having problems. I mean take imperialism. This fuckin country makes up one-sixteenth of the world population and owns or controls 55 per cent of its natural resources. That was enough to know about imperialism it seemed to me. As for racism, well once in Mississippi we were taking a medical survey door-to-door and I remember the mothers would all say their children were all "doin jus fine" and I'd look down and see twelve-year-old black kids with teeth totally rotted away — they thought that was "normal" health. The woman would ask you if you'd like something to drink and you knew it would be ice water and that white people up North would call that "soul" but you called it poverty. About working-class exploitation, well that meant working one summer in Wyman-Gordon's airplane factory getting oil in your lungs when they sprayed the 55,000-ton press and having your mind fall out from working the swing shift. I couldn't understand why Revolutionary Youth Movement Number Two or for that matter, Revolutionary Youth Movement Number One, was reluctant to organize youth into a revolutionary movement. Well who am I to say. I haven't read Marx in years and when you get right down to it I'm too sloppy a thinker to be in the vanguard. Anyway it's more fun in the back of the bus. When we were young it was always the best place to get laid.

These are some of the thoughts I pondered while looking at the road with field glasses ready to wake everyone up Paul Revere-style with shouts of "The Pigs are coming." I had no idea of what SDS was into but there was that image again of a row of high-powered cameras in the third-floor window across the street from their convention. There was the FBI in heavy numbers guarding the NATIONAL SECURITY and all that other gung-ho shit. SDS ain't LSD but it ain't FBI either. I guess that's a way of saying, "enemies of my enemies are my friends," which is said a lot at conferences these days and argued about these nights. I wondered what LSDSDS spelled...

Our little underground get-together on a Michigan farm had more gentle vibes. No one shouted, "Beware he who waves his long hair to oppose his long hair." I wondered behind which tree the FBI secret cameras lurked. I didn't want to get too paranoid, but fuck, there were the White Panthers guarding the road with shotguns. Melvin Newsreel was monitoring police calls and translating the numbers into words using a little card (all you need is a simple UHF modifier and you can get the code breakdown in any good criminology book in a large library). There were about thirty of us on defense patrol ready to put into operation Plan B to fight the Pigs if they returned. We had about twenty or so weapons, an escape route, and well I just didn't know what the fuck I'd do if they came back. It would be as good a place as any and as good a reason as any to blast my first Pig. I wondered what kind of a jolt the shotgun would give. It was sure a pretty piece.

Oh yeah, I forgot to lay it on you about why all this people's militia stuff is going on. Well this afternoon in the middle of a discussion on political repression we looked up and there were about seventy local Pigs with riot helmets and shotguns running through the woods in some complicated green beret-type maneuver. We all were forced to sort of line up while doors to the farmhouse were smashed in and a half-ass search was conducted. I kept wondering whether the Pigs were concerned about Liberation News Service (politicos) or Tate Blues Band (hippies) and things like that. When the Pigs left we had a heavy rap session about self-defense, land, and whether or not the chickens bar-be-cuing on the open fire were done yet. Skip Taub laid out a heavy rap about what was coming down in the Ann Arbor area like Pigs shaving longhairs, searching cars at drive-ins, hassling young people in a whole lot of ways and not allowing rock music in the park. I listened careful to Skip—more careful than I had listened to anyone in a long time. In Ann Arbor they were working out the mixing of revolutionary outlaws and cultural nationalists. I was thinking about rock and what the Yippies had tried to pull off in Chicago and I thought about the scared Pigs stuttering as they quivered with shotguns in their hands facing the defiant hippies just an hour ago. I thought about standing in People's Park, most beautiful spot on earth, and listening to Frank Bardacke and Stu Albert* run down the plan to rip off the land from the university and suck Reagan into a fight. In Chicago I felt that I was ready to die over our right to be in Lincoln Park and how defending liberated land meant more than Vietnam. **The only way to support a revolution is to make your own.** But most of all I thought about land and self-defense. I made a note to check into the Woodstock Ventures operation as soon as I hit New York. Those promoters were into some heavy shit, all right. Half the people at the conference thought the festival was going to take place on Bob Dylan's farm. Bob Dylan's farm? It wasn't even taking place in Woodstock!

*Stu, one of the founders of the Yippie Empire, is currently doing ninety days in a California jail. At least thirty per cent of the key Yippie people in Chicago are now in jail. Most of the others face a number of trials.

To Anita

(Written under temperature of 104 and very yellow hep)

Anita glows
   sitting legs crossed in corner
threading a needle contemplating
   eternal truthniks
what mysterious jujubes of ecstasy
lie within the yummy texture
of her brow?
   A little tuft of hair juts out casting
her face forward ... Chinese
princess from some early Ting-Tong
Dynasty.
Oh if I could only plunge my rough
and aching tongue through those dreamy
lips — luscious sensuous lips of 1942
Betty Grable calendar. Yum-yum.
Neck perfect form on which to perch
this smiling face of a laughing bird.
(I pause for a sip on my ice cream soda
and continue down her back)...

Outline
Yippie! Movie *

1. Daley face on a gong. Long-hair girl whacks the gong. "The Yippies' Answer to Mayor Daley."
2. Burial of Yippie leader. "On Christmas Eve 1967, Yippie born. Died that night." Solemn procession singing "The First Yippie (Noel)." Humming ... Throw Coffin out of window.
3. Typical Yippie meetings and personalities. Billy the Kid, Marilyn Monroe, Franz Kafka. Shots

from old movies of mass happenings — especially war films — interspersed with Pentagon, running in street demonstrations, Grand Central Station Massacre, huge shot of April '66 rally with 400,000. Narrator; "this infinitesimal group of hard-core agitators ..." Sequence ends with shot of Klan riding in from "Birth of a Nation." Phil Ochs' new song for background.

*This film was made as an answer to Mayor Daley's epic "What Trees Do They Plant?" It was shown on WNEW-TV in New York. Ed Sanders did the final editing with Mark Newsreel, Keith Lampe and Paul Krassner did the dialogue. Its budget came to about twelve dollars once we had stolen everything we needed. Film available from Newsreel, 322 7th Ave., New York, N.Y.

4. Chicago Massacre Shots and Wolfe Lowenthal Folk Song. Banjo (Rennie Davis) in background. "Mayor Daley Shoot to Kill" speech.

5. Cops, billyclubs, blood, large hookah. Cops come home from hard day of clubbing. Greeted by wives. Take off clothes and puff hookah. "We'll return to the Revolution after this word..." Advertisement for Yippie helmets done by Marshall Efron.

6. Flashy red, white and blue chorus singing "He's a Grand Ol Pig" and tap dancing. (Use Fillmore Stage.)

7. Pignic and Procession. Shots of people eating free ham sandwiches and marching from Gansevoort garbage dump to Tompkins Square Park.

60

8. Shots of headlines about Chicago flash rapidly. Shot of Pig eating newspapers ... flashes VOTE PIG IN '68.

9. Shots of Daley, Humphrey, Nixon, Agnew, Wallace, Martha Raye, Pearl Mesta, cops' faces, Mamie Eisenhower, Christine Jorgensen, etc., interspersed with close-ups of Pig faces. Lots of Oinks! and Grunts! and Oinks!

10. a) Funny sequence-shot of kid sneaking along sidewalk; scribbles picture of Pig face on bank window ... and sneaks off into the sunset.
b) Shots of people going into voting booths interspersed with people taking showers — and other nutty things — e.g. running out of building with voting machine. Sneaking into pay toilet shot. Shots of Jews entering Dachau, hog-calling contest and Democratic Convention.
Heavy Pig Chorale at end with Times Square thing.

61

Free John Sinclair

> There ain't no law in America only the honkie
> power structure.

John Sinclair, July 28, 1969 just before sentencing.

John Sinclair is a huge lover with masses of curly black hair flowing all over his head and shoulders. John is a mountain of a man. He can fuck twenty times a day and fight like a wild bear. He and his White Panther brothers and sisters from Ann Arbor, Michigan, are the most alive force in the whole Midwest. They turn on thousands of kids each week to their own beauty and build them into warriors and artists of the new Nation. For this John Sinclair was entrapped into giving two joints of grass to two undercover Pigs. For this some bald-headed judge named Columbo sentenced John Sinclair to nine-and-a-half to ten years in the penitentiary at Jackson, Michigan. For this the same courts are waiting to put on trial Pun Plamondon, John's closest brother and Minister of Defense of the Party, for handing a free joint to another undercover Pig. For this they want to send Pun away for twenty years to life in the same penitentiary on a phony charge of dispensing marijuana without a prescription.*

The kids in Ann Arbor are coming together. Resistance is growing to the practice of Pigs cutting off kids' hair, of breaking up free rock concerts in the park, of raiding communes and harassing underground newspapers. In Ann Arbor, the kids are learning karate. In Ann Arbor, the women know how to handle shotguns. In Ann Arbor, the freaks are organizing petition drives to recall the Head Pig Sheriff Harvey. In Ann Arbor, the hip community takes on the cops in pitched street battles. In Ann Arbor, they are prepared to build and defend the

---

*Pun, Jeannie, Magdelene Sinclair, John's expectant wife, and two other White Panthers were just arrested in New Jersey when they left WOODSTOCK NATION. It was one of those typically unconstitutional car searches the Pigs across the country have been making famous. They claimed they found a little guess what? Contributions should be sent to the John Sinclair Defense Fund, 1510 Hill St., Ann Arbor, Michigan.

Nation by any means necessary. In Ann Arbor and in other places like that around the country they ain't into peace and music, they're into WAR and MUSIC and Right on! Music can make the walls shake but you need an army to take the city and artists to rebuild it. Rock music will provide the energy but the people will provide the power, for only with power can we defend what beauty we create ....

Up in Woodstock a big thing was made of how you could sit around and smoke right out in the open. A questionnaire prepared by Deputy Inspector Joe Fink (you remember good ol Vanguard Capitalism Joe, don't you?), of the Lower East Side or rather the East Village; when he sends off his men to pound the shit out of the street people he does it in the Lower East Side where we live. When he talks to the establishment press he does it in the East Village. Anyway, one of the key questions on the form to recruit four hundred off-duty New York policemen for security at the festival went like this:

Question: What do you do if someone blows marijuana smoke in your face?

Wrong Answer: Arrest him.

Right Answer: Smile and inhale.

That was up in Woodstock and that was because the cops were bought off. In PIG NATION, it doesn't work like that at all, no sir, not at all! In PIG NATION last year there were 250,000 narcotics arrests mostly for grass. They have trained dogs in Detroit for shipment around the country to sniff out the stuff. They have increased the penalties to fascist proportions. They have used pot busts as an excuse to attack WOODSTOCK NATION. Nixon's three biggest enemies right now are the Vietcong, blacks and drugs. Drugs means us and he treats us like the country has always treated its VIETCONG NIGGERS. He aims to kick our ass.

Napalming villages in Vietnam is not the only kind of imperialism the country is into and trying to land the drug people in the clink like blacks is not the only way Nixon makes war, not the only way by far ...   63

The Great Grass Famine

There's so much shit up here, no wonder there
ain't none anyplace else.

Ann Fettamen
Underground writer,
WOODSTOCK NATION

This is probably the first time this story has ever been told — pieces have been told but not this much. In the kind of work I do, I meet a lot of big dope dealers. Like I mean big ones. They get their kicks out of the Yippies as much as do the heads of the Rock Empire. They also help about as much. Once in a while they'll give a little free dope like for the Valentine's Day Marijuana Massacre, which cannot even be discussed, but they'll never give anything big and they'll never give any money — not one thin dime. The relationship has always been a strange one. They are after all capitalists, but then, too, they are outlaws. For the most part, they admire PIG NATION in the way the Mafia does, but, like the Mafia, they probably have a better picture of the corruptness of the institutions that rule the society than most people.* It takes a crook to know a crook and the dope dealers are well-qualified social critics. Their information should always be given a certain amount of respect. Because of that attitude, I've been able to meet some very heavy dealers, like the guy who produced most of the STP in the world and has a network of ten laboratories. Or the cat who got caught with sixty-seven million dollars worth of acid and beat the rap which is always the case with the big guys. I ain't met Owsley but I've met the guy who turned on Leary and the guy who turned on everyone for free in Chicago. The weirdest of them all is my buddy who we'll call "Frankie." Frankie has been dealing for six years without a bust. When I first met him he was pushing the stuff out of a hot-dog push-cart on St. Mark's Place. Frankie used to scoot around the Lower East Side, wheelin and dealin with a nervous little gesture that I never saw anybody else master. Frankie was the only guy that could look

*When I speak of dope I don't speak of heroin and other hard drugs. Given this exception the Mafia is almost totally absent from the dope world. Their interests lie in other areas and other dealers have filled the vacuum.

over both shoulders at the same time.

Today Frankie is real big-time. He arranges the biggest deals in the East. When he was called to see Tommie Ryan, Mafia boss of the bosses, Tommie flicked Frankie's long hair with the back of his hand, "What's dis for, keed?" "Oh, it's good for business," replied Frankie, without batting an eye. If the Mafia wanted to fuck with Frankie they could wipe him out but for now anyway it was hands off. Frankie was part of a syndicate or brotherhood, one of the seven or eight top ones that controlled the grass market. From about 1964 to 1967 when grass really started to take off, most of the dealing was individual hustlin and some Mafia stuff. About two years ago certain dealers who had been gettin pretty good at it started banding together in mutual protective societies. It was the time for big mergers just like down on Wall Street. California had about the biggest but New York was plenty big. Big pot deals were made that involved tons of grass and hundreds of thousands of dollars. Slowly a GRASS EMPIRE began to emerge that had control of the market. Covering the market meant sewing up the huge pot fields in Mexico cause Mexico was where most of the grass comes from. Mexico was where the government and the customs inspectors were all bought off. Mexico was just across the border.

In the spring of '68 the government began to poke its nose around the pot fields along the western coast of Mexico. Down around Acapulco and Mazatlán on the Gulf of California where the big maestro (pot plantation owner) action was all going to the syndicates. Seems they wanted to try and sabotage a few deals and burn a few fields to cool out the border shipments. The Mexican government, too, put pressure on the plantations because the Olympics were coming in and Mexico wanted the world to dig its tequila, not its Acapulco Gold. It was nothing real heavy though the price of a key in one-thousand-ton lots went from fifty to seventy-five dollars and drove the street price in the U.S. from one hundred to two hundred dollars per single key.*

When Nixon came to Washington waving the law-and-odor banner, the Federal Bureau of Narcotics was one of the first agencies to interest him. He announced in his very first speech, his inaugural address if I remember right, that he was adding three hundred new narks to the team. That would now make about one nark for every twenty thousand heads, so a policy of simply busting cats on the corner was not the only thing that had to be done. The Narcotics Bureau ran down to Nixon and Attorney General Mitchell, who just gotta be allergic to grass, the BIG PLAN. That plan, which was already proving somewhat effective, was to nip pot in the bud. It was back to Mexico in the spring, with a lot more deals with the Mexican government, and a lot more chemical defoliants.

Not even the rich syndicates could outbid Uncle Sam, especially when he was drunk with imperialist determination. The maestros didn't give a shit and laid huge fields of pot on Uncle Sam, the way Senator Eastland laid on nonexistent fields of cotton. Agents shelled out the bread and proceeded to wipe out almost the entire crop. The syndicates had some stored on this side of the border, usually in heavy barrels buried in the ground, but it was nothing much at all. The price rose higher and higher. By August keys were bringing one hundred twenty-five dollars on the wholesale market in one-thousand-ton lots and a lot of hassle because the whole border operation was demanding bigger and bigger rake-offs. In New York City a key was going for as high as six-fifty and the

---

*A key means kilo or 2.2 pounds, about the size and shape of a brick when compressed. The U.S. prices quoted vary from region to region and fluctuate with the season, supply, and the amount of local heat.

price was expected to hit a thousand dollars by the end of the year.

Grass wasn't the only dope in trouble. Hashish started to fill the vacuum left by the grass famine but the narks, finding it impossible to do business in the Middle-East, tightened up customs inspections and began to use more foreign informers. Big hash busts, especially in the East, were becoming the order of the day. Large mescaline shipments were also being intercepted.

What the government was doing was to drive organic dope off the market! Ridalin, LSD, THC, DMT, synthetic mescaline, amphetamines, anything that could be made into a pill, anything that was synthetic was in for good. There were plenty of pills and plenty more to come. They were less bulky than the organics. Many were quasi-legal and they could be manufactured inside the borders or smuggled in without much hassle. The government would find it harder to build up pressure against the synthetics seeing as how about two out of five Amerikans were going up or coming down with some kind of pill every day. The profits were mighty good on the pills and besides with the speed (amphetamine) family the users often got addicted, making more permanent customers. So what if the pills produced more aggressive, violent, self-destructive behavior! So what if pills got you hooked! It was the most amazing development in the dope culture since the emergence of LSD. We were turning into a nation of Speed Freaks and Nixon, the used-car dealer from Whittier, California, was becomin the biggest pill pusher of them all!!!

69

Woodstock or Bust

Just to give you a rundown of where my head was at when I set off to the WOODSTOCK NATION, let me give you the year's rundown on my busts. If it wasn't for my lawyer, Jerry Lefcourt, I'd be hallucinating this from some jail cell rather than the floor of a Random House office.

1. Early in August '68, resisting arrest added to a charge of criminal trespassing during Columbia revolt filed a full three months earlier! Trial begins September 4th.

2. August 27, 1968, Chicago — for having "Fuck" on forehead and resisting arrest. (Fifteen days and one-year probation for resisting. "Fuck" dismissed on the grounds that you cannot offend the morals of a policeman — resisting charge is on appeal.)

3. September 13. While returning to Chicago to stand trial on the above charges, arrested with lawyer for non-appearance in court. (Dismissed)

4. Later that day, arrested again in Chicago for possessing a concealed weapon (state charge). (Dismissed when prosecuting attorneys found it impossible to produce said concealed weapon.)

5. And still later the same day, by the Federal Bureau of Investigation, and charged with crimes aboard an aircraft. (Dismissed but not before they confined me to the District of Manhattan for three months and made me spend a lot of bread zipping in and out of Chicago for hearings.)

6. October — HUAC hearing in Washington. Busted for wearing an Amerikan flag shirt. (Facing thirty days. Appeal rejected by District Court of Appeals, Washington, D.C. and headed for the Supreme Court.) When I was arrested, I got an almost fatal case of serum hepatitis when prison guards took a blood sample, under force, with a dirty needle. I currently have a $300,000 lawsuit pending against the U.S. Government. (Now the busts are interrupted cause

I'm laid up three months with hep.)
7. Somewhere in the sky between Buffalo and Rochester last February, busted for not fastening my seat belt. Finally resulted in charge of disorderly conduct (dismissed). On at least three occasions airlines have refused to fly me and on Amerikan Airlines they have this strange habit of searching my bags. Needless to say, I had to give my five youth cards away.
8. In March, indicted for conspiracy with intent to incite riots, etc., in Chicago. Trial begins September 24th. Hope you'll drop around or write us at the

Conspiracy Office in Chicago.*

9. Later that same night busted for possession of loaded automatics, heroin, blackjacks and other assorted goodies "found in a community office."

(All but possession of loaded automatics have been dropped. Trial begins September 8th. The interesting thing about this bust is that I was not there at the time of arrest and the office, which is next door to the police station, is not even in my name. What do you think my grandmother said when she read about this one?)

10. In April — felonious assault against two cops while in court on the Columbia hearing. I was pulled out of a phone booth in the lobby when some keen-eyed Pig recognized me and clubbed me to the floor. Also added to this charge was obstructing government business, disturbing the peace, resisting arrest and disorderly conduct. Trial begins November 15th.

All this amounts to more time in prison than I care to imagine and endless hearings and bail hassles ... Lenny Bruce once said that in the halls of justice the only justice was in the halls. I learned something on that last bust. Lenny was wrong. There isn't even any justice in the halls.

*We just learned today that we are almost certain to be locked into the trial date. Judge Julius Hoffman is determined to fry us. He has refused all of our motions for dismissal and postponements, even though our two chief counsels probably can't be in court by mid-September. Charles Garry is in the hospital and faces a murder trial when he gets out. William Kunstler has the Panther 21 conspiracy case, the Bob Williams murder case, and two heavy Rap Brown trials all in September.

Bobby Seale, I guess you know, was just arrested on a conspiracy to commit murder rap and other charges and might have difficulties making the date. Jerry Rubin has thirty days to do in California and I've got the two trials coming up next week.... By the time we hit trial we might be the Chicago Two. The judge threw out three spectators from the courtroom today because their dress was "an affront to the dignity of the court." He said, "The defendants can wear anything they want, even come naked, but the spectators must respect the court." Well, seeing as how we have nothing to hide ...

73

YOUTH MAKES
THE REVOLUTION
BE STRONG
BE BEAUTIFUL

TOM HAYDEN
ABBIE HOFFM
2 P.M. MONDAY APRIL 7 UN

The Hard Rain's Already Fallin'*

> You're either part of the solution or part of
> the problem.
>> Eldridge Cleaver

> He not busy being born, is busy dying.
>> Bob Dylan

Someday real soon we're going to see posters in the post office that say "WANTED FOR CONSPIRACY TO INCITE RIOT" and there smiling out at us will be pictures of our favorite rock groups. Unreal? Well, maybe you're not hip to what's been going down lately. The Law-and-Odor apes and this senile dinosaur we call a government have flipped out. Preventive detention, the no-knock clause in the new drug laws, appointment of Burger and Haynsworth to the Supreme Court, and the extensive use of wiretapping by the Justice Department are all part of a wave of repression.

Over three hundred Black Panthers are now in jail as a result of a nation-wide plot to destroy their organization. White radicals are being arrested. Underground newspapers are being harassed. G.I.s who speak out are receiving harsh sentences. The police have been unleashed. Last summer in Chicago, it was clubs and tear gas; in Berkeley this spring it was shotguns and buckshot.

*This article was written for the free program that was handed out in WOODSTOCK. It's a liberal piece with no swears or no bad English. Thank-you, ma'm.

The hard rain's already fallin and it isn't just the politicos that are getting wet. Read the list: Jimi Hendrix, MC 5, The Who, Phil Ochs, Tim Buckley, Jefferson Airplane, Grateful Dead, Jim Morrison, Creedence Clearwater, the Turtles, Moby Grape, Ray Charles, The Fugs, Dave Van Ronk, Joan Baez — all have been busted recently. Busted because the authorities want to destroy our cultural revolution in the same way they want to destroy our political revolution. Maybe the man can't bust our music but he sure as hell can bust our musicians. If the government wanted to, it could bust rock groups on charges of conspiracy to incite riot. Last year Congress passed an anti-riot act which made it illegal to urge people to go to an event at which a riot later occurs. The law makes it illegal to *travel from state to state, write letters or telegrams, speak on the radio or television, make a telephone call* with the *intention* of encouraging people to participate in a *riot*. A *riot* meaning *an act of violence occurring in an assemblage of three or more persons.* The people doing the urging never have to commit an act of violence or know the people who do. They never, in fact, have to urge a riot. William Kunstler, famed constitutional lawyer, feels "rock-and-roll stars and promoters could be prosecuted under this law if violence occurred at a show."

The law is currently being tested in the upcoming trial of eight movement activists: Rennie Davis, Dave Dellinger, John Froines, Tom Hayden, Jerry Rubin, Bobby Seale, Lee Weiner, and myself, all participants in the demonstrations last August in Chicago. You remember Chicago, where the facade of a democratically run convention was washed down the streets with the blood of young people. The Whole World Was Watching and what it saw was what the official Walker Report later termed a "police riot." Richard Nixon wants to put an end to demonstrations. Mayor Daley wants revenge. They have decided to set an example for anyone who speaks out against the government by putting us in prison for ten years.

None of us are shedding any tears about our upcoming trial. In a sense the indictments are like receiving an academy award for our work. Many of us have already done time in jail, we have been arrested and beaten numerous times, we have lived with the FBI following us and monitoring our phone calls. For us personally the trial is just a part of our activity in the movement. When you get down to it, we *are* guilty of being members of a vast conspiracy. A conspiracy pitted against the war in Vietnam and the government that still perpetuates that war, against the oppression of black communities, against the harassment of our cultural revolution, against an educational system that seeks only to channel us into a society we see as corrupt and impersonal, against the growing police state, and finally against the dehumanizing work roles that a capitalist economic system demands. What we are for, quite simply, is a total revolution. We are for a society in which the people directly decide and control the decisions that affect their lives. We are for people's power or as one or our brothers in Berkeley put it, "soulful socialism." In the past few years our numbers have grown from hundreds to millions of young people. Our conspiracy has grown more militant. Flower children have lost their innocence and grown their thorns. We have recognized that our culture in order to survive must be defended. Furthermore we have realized that the revolution is more than digging rock or turning on. The revolution is about coming together in a struggle for change. It is about the destruction of a system based on bosses and competition and the building of a new community based on people and cooperation. That old system is dying all around us and we joyously come out in the streets to dance on its grave. With our free stores, liberated buildings, communes, people's parks, dope, free bodies and our music, we'll build our society in the vacant lots of the old and we'll do it by any means necessary. Right On!

77

A Question of Intent

The Chicago Eight are probably the most no
conspiring conspiracy ever hatched and yet we we
going down. The actual charge was "Conspiracy
cross state lines with intent to incite riot" and t
key word was "intent." It's all a question of "intent
the judge will say, and the jury will look over at
nasty eight and come down hard, for the jury w
have a difficult time drawing a line between intent

overthrow the government, intent to incite riot, intent to be black, intent to help the Vietnamese keep their land, intent to give LSD to everyone who wants it and intent to live in a family of man. At times I think I'll just scream out something like "Guilty Due to Sanity" and give the judge the "fuck you" sign. It's going to be such an ordeal sitting still in that cracker court for four months, sort of like being back in school. What if we get gunned down in the streets — Chicago Mafia-style, say around Hallowe'en??? The Great Hallowe'en Massacre the papers will say ... "It was too bad they couldn't get their day in court but how do we know they didn't provoke the shooting? How do we know they didn't *intend* it to happen this way?" So you see when you hear about this heavy trial coming down in Chicago and all the wild stories coming out of it, just roll that question of intent around in your mind ... roll it around too when you consider the case of the Woodstock Four.* They crossed state lines. They created a dangerous situation. They incited people to riot. They are helping to create a culture which is in violent clash with the parent culture. They manipulated the media and lured people with promises of music so they could carry out their wild drug orgies. How come they're not charged under the anti-riot law and facing ten years like those of us who conspired to have a Festival of Life in Chicago? That's a heavy question. Let's examine part of the case against them — or for them, depending on whether or not you want to see the government overthrown.

*The four promoters of Woodstock Ventures are Michael Lang, Artie Kornfeld, Joel Rosenman and John Roberts. All are in their mid-twenties. Lang was a big dealer and owned a head shop in Coral Gables until he got the idea for Woodstock Ventures. Kornfeld was a rock promoter for such bubble rock groups as the Cowsills. Rosenman and Roberts had the bread. Roberts' old man owned a multi-million-dollar pharmaceutical firm. The other day when he was in the bank declaring bankruptcy, his father rushed in with his aide, wrote a check for one million dollars and exclaimed, "No son of mine will go bankrupt. You can lose your money again and again but your name only once."

Government Exhibit A

Ladies and gentlemen of the jury, I ask you to consider the first piece of evidence, this ad that appeared in hundreds of newspapers throughout the eastern half of the United States. Is this ad, is the image evoked in this ad, one of peace and music? Do you really think the Woodstock Four really love the good people of Wallkill? Good people like you and me. Why are they pictured as grotesque monsters? Why the guns? Why the play on WALLKILL like up against the WALL! and KILL! — favorite chants of the same wild anarchists that brought shame to the fair city of Chicago. The government maintains that this ad is a device to create a nation *intent* on destroying our beloved PIG NATION. For example, notice how they encourage the use of marijuana, a drug, which according to the Narcotics Abuse and Control Center of Florida, may produce chromosome damage. Notice the phrase "and twice as much grass." Grass, in the vernacular of these sordid degenerates, is synonymous with marijuana. Notice the phrase "we decided we'd rather switch now and fight Wallkill later." Fight! I ask you to consider ladies and gentlemen of the jury whether the intent of these people who you sit in judgment on really was to have three days of peace and music?

Government Exhibit B

2-Hour Movie

Ladies and gentlemen, as you watch the following film we want you to pay close attention to scenes of flagrant drug taking. We want you to consider the carefully phrased announcements from the stage — by one MR. CHIP MONCK, listed as a co-conspirator — which blatantly encouraged the use of drugs. We want you to pay attention to the scene of a young man putting mustard on his draft card and letting his girl friend, who has no bra on I might add, take a bite out of it as if it were some sort of salami sandwich! We ask you also to notice the banners praising Che Guevara, Ho Chi Minh, Huey Newton and other foreign enemies of PIG NATION. We know the defense will claim the political revolutionaries responsible for those banners were not connected with the festival, but we have proof that we will later present to show that large amounts of money were exchanged with said political groups. We ask you to notice the supposed "cure" for bad LSD experiences which consisted of having people engage in nothing less than mass fornication! Fornication, ladies and gentlemen, and these were thirteen-year-old children ... Our children!

Finally, we ask you to think of the good people of Wallkill and Bethlehem, excuse me Bethel, and the havoc brought upon their peaceful communities ... we ask you ladies and gentlemen of the jury to stand up for PIG NATION. We call upon you to defend everything this country holds sacred. We call upon you to find the Woodstock Four guilty of conspiracy to incite riot .... Thank you for your patience.

WANTED

REWARD

Smack Dab in the
Middle
of
the
Monster

Bethel, N. Y.: You sit on the big stage watered by the blue spotlights while the Big Pink Band plays Bob Dylan's "I Shall Be Released" and you look out into the eyes of the monster.

Alfred C. Aronowitz, New York *Post*

On Saturday night up on the stage you felt the monster was going to crush the Amerikan Dinosaur. You could see the distant bonfires on far-off hills and sense thousands of soldiers resurrected from the Macedonian army hammering out their weapons. You looked at say two hundred thousand or so heads who had crawled out of the catacombs in PIG NATION. 85

They were all piled up on People Hill and saw the spotlight eyes burn down on Creedence Clearwater, hypnotizing them, driving them into an orgiastic fury that shook the whole motherfuckin stage. It felt like the last scene from "Frankenstein" performed by the Living Theatre, that busload of hippy nuns that breezed through a while back. I had seen them do "Frankenstein" at MIT and I lay my hand on the scaffolding and felt it shake with the fury of the gods. It was just before the FBI grabbed me in Cambridge and I had to fly immediately back to Chicago and face a hearing on why I jumped jurisdiction to go see the Living Theatre and my two sick kids. The whole motherfuckin stage at Woodstock was shakin like that as it slipped back and forth in two feet of mud. Every once in a while a straight dude from the Construction Company or the Safety Department or something like that would rush up to someone who looked like he was in charge and yell "We must stop this! The stage will collapse! Everybody must get off!" And always some shaggy-haired freak would hug him and say "Swingin baby, we're gonna fly up here forever!" and the swingers and the faith healers and the astrology freaks were all right that Saturday night up there. That was one of the eerie things about the WOOD-STOCK NATION, every nut in it was right, even the Meher Baba buffs.

I'd run back and forth to the stage boppin across this bridge over Lake Shore Drive* — the shortest way

*Lake Shore Drive was also the name of the huge outer drive that surrounds Lincoln Park in Chicago and if you dig on its initials you swear the whole fuckin country is haunted.

To get around fast as all hell you only had to know a few passwords, master a few scribbly signatures, shout and have a look of masterful determination that said, "If I don't get in here, the whole festival could collapse, people will be crushed to death, heads will roll." You ought to practice this look and manner. If you had mastered these techniques, then you would have found out a lot of shit like about exclusive deals with *Look* magazine (if you wanted to take still pictures) and with Wadley Productions (if you were into shooting films).

86

from the Field Hospital to the Monster. You had to run down a hill past the whirling helicopter hurricanes, past the performers pavilion. You then had to show a crumpled card that said "Admit to stage OK M. Lang." I had practiced forging Mike Lang's name for about ten minutes the day before but found out it was rarely necessary to be good at it; usually flashing my Identification Card (which I had drawn myself) at an usher would do the trick. Besides the word was out that I was running the Field Hospital. And even in Hippie Heaven broken bones and freak-outs mean something, at least most times they do. So I had a pretty easy time getting on the stage and would bring these slips up to Chip Monck or John Morris who was an old friend from backstage at the Fillmore East. The slips were an attempt to communicate some serious medical information to the Monster. I'll run down a few of them and give you Chip Monck's translations so you'll get the contrast. You should really read the directions like a school teacher just before air-raid practice, and the translations like you were pouring molasses while on two caps of mescaline listening to the Incredible String Band murmuring in the closet.

You would have known you could pull up to Ken's American Gas Station in White Lake and say, "Charge it to Woodstock Ventures," and sign any name you wanted, even George Metesky. If you really felt zonked and dirty you could have written on a slip of paper "Good for 1 shower" and signed Stan Freedman's name and used it at the El Monaco Motel. You would have known, most importantly, that there were no official slips of paper for messages so you could write it on anything. You would also have known that ripping off a walkie-talkie was pretty easy and with that you could have immediately had all kinds of personnel and equipment at your disposal. All this and more was necessary to know. For knowing this kind of information was how you survived in the jungles of electronic chaos. Compared to Chicago, stealing information and using it up at Woodstock was like catching kisses thrown by Tiny Tim. The only difference was that the government was trying to hang ten years on you for knowing too much about Chicago and up here you were turning into Mr. Florence Nightingale of the Flower Children.

DON'T DRINK THE WATER IN THE POND BEHIND THE HOGFARM CAMP UNLESS YOU PUT SOME CHLORINE IN IT. TWO DROPS TO THE GALLON.

Lay off water, man, it's a real bummer.

THERE ARE NOW NINE FIRST AID CENTERS ESTABLISHED. FOR FIRST AID TREATMENT GO FIRST TO EITHER THE CENTER IN THE HOGFARM SITE OR THE CENTER AT THE TOP OF THE HILL BEHIND THE CENTRAL INFORMATION BOOTH. VERY BAD INJURIES SHOULD REPORT TO THE FIELD HOSPITAL IN THE PINK AND WHITE TENTS ACROSS THE ROAD.

We got a lot of groovy hospitals stashed away. Bummers to the Yellow Tent at the top of the hill or over there (waving arms). Heavy stuff to the pink and white tents.

Remember now these announcements are being made to something like say 400,000 people, for as you might not have realized, WOODSTOCK NATION was by Saturday the second-largest city in New York and I think the tenth largest in the country.*

Well you want to know something about those announcements? They worked! Such was the mystical power of the microphones and public address system and so tuned in were all the 400,000 or 500,000 or 1,000,000, depending on where you drew the

---

*WOODSTOCK NATION was shaped like a huge guitar with the body around Bethel and the neck extending about ten miles down Route 17B. Also there were reports of people jammed on the New York Thruway and in bus stations and airports all over the country. San Francisco International Airport reported turning away close to one thousand people headed to Woodstock on Friday. The Port Authority Bus Terminal in New York by Saturday had called it quits. The

national boundaries, that everyone knew where to go. There were other happenings up there on the stage, psychic games with Artie Kornfeld and Mike Lang, two of the Woodstock Four. "Hey Mike, chaos has a certain beauty to it, doesn't it?" I suggest. We played little games up there as I tried to get them into the morality-politico bag and they tried to get me to drop out and join them on their trip. They made all sorts of promises and liked me an awful lot especially once I decided to make the Florence Nightingale scene. They were shrewd motherfuckers and probably ripped me off as much as me them. After all, I was setting up the hospital for free! Certainly they fared much better than the Chicago authorities in our bouts — in fact to be honest they knocked me on my ass a few times, but maybe that was due to all the drugs I had taken and maybe it was due to how I was having the first bad acid trip I'd had in four years. Maybe we ought to get into that right now since it really is a gas and I been waiting all this time to lay the story on you cause it was the wildest fucker ever. Wilder than pissing on the Pentagon, wilder than standing in front of a Washington judge, half-naked with a Vietcong flag painted on my back, wilder than throwin out money at the Stock Exchange, wilder than fuckin in the middle of Lincoln Park when the tear gas came rollin in — this was one of the wildest ever. Let's get into it. I'm gonna try this next song left-handed cause my fingers hurt like crazy from writing. It's 5:00 a.m. and I've been at it for a lot of hours.

Roger and out.

promoters spent a good deal of time both Friday and Saturday holding press conferences urging people not to come. State troopers along the New York Thruway, which was forced to close part of the time, re-routed tens of thousands into different areas of upstate New York. There were probably as many people turned away as finally made it close enough to say "I was there."

Power is the ability to make matter act in a desired manner.

Huey or Isaac Newton

We will have to wait and see if the Monster decides to move. As long as it stays in the valley we'll be out of danger.

"It Came From Outer Space"

When I left Chicago I felt we had won a great victory. The lines between "us," the people in the streets, and "them," the people in authority, had been clearly established, the police had seen to that. With a small number of people we had been able to successfully do damage to a huge and powerful political party. Some people even say our action and the mess we created was chiefly responsible for the defeat of Humphrey. I'm not sure; I'm not sure why things happen in PIG NATION, I'm too much involved with trying to fuck the Statue of Liberty to be able to give intelligent overviews. Leaving Woodstock I was not so sure of what exactly had happened. Figuring out who was the enemy was not only difficult but the mere posing of the question seemed out of place. There were so many contradictions and ambiguities like Jimi Hendrix, who literally wraps his long-hair black legs around his guitar and fucks it into ecstasy, playing "The Star Spangled Banner," New York City cops (one I recognized as the guy who busted me on the gun charge) in scarlet jackets with peace signs, hospitals in bright-colored circus tents, please chiefs instead of police chiefs, straight dudes like office secretaries and shoe salesmen and teachers getting their minds blown out and ending up swimmin naked in the lake or fuckin in the grass or tryin acid for the first time. There were some who turned into gods. There were people who cried out in ecstasy and people who did nothing but smile the whole time. It was a hell-of-a-mess allright. I mean aside from the fact that they'll make great movie scenes, can you attach any revolutionary significance to the following?

91

Chasidic Jews and Catholic nuns giving away free food while people across the street charge twenty-five cents for a glass of water.

Bob Wolf standing there totally naked interviewing an eighty-five-year-old lady resident of Bethel for *The Realist*.

A guy right out of the Bible with a sign saying "Don't Kill Animals" followed by a sheep.

A long-haired guy dealing acid from the back of a horse.

The staff of a large mass-media magazine plotting to take pictures of themselves naked, blur them up a bit and get it on the cover of their own magazine.

Rows and rows of tents for at least thirty miles down Route 17B and into the N. Y. Thruway.

There were hundreds and hundreds more flashes that one saw. And then there was the immensity of the crowd. God, how can you capture the feeling of being with 400,000 people and everyone being stoned on something? Were we pilgrims or lemmings? Was this really the beginning of a new civilization or the symptom of a dying one? Were we establishing a liberated zone or entering a detention camp? Like dig it baby. When the Jews entered the ovens at Dachau, the Nazis played hip Wagner music, passed out flowers and handed out free bars of soap. That's right Hippies, take your clothes off, we are all goin to ze big fuck-in ... zat's right ... we are all gonna groove mit da showers ... ya ya ... by the way would you mind it if we pulled your teeth out ... just step over here kinda. That's nice ... be boppa do." Heh, there certainly are a lot of questions that come to mind. You could sure come away pessimistic about the future of the MONSTER. You could sure have legitimate doubts about WOODSTOCK NATION ...
But!!!

And now I call upon myself to vote and I vote

THUMBS UP! Right on! And I'm happy and smilin. Cocksure of the future and rememberin the great scene that Anita told me about how this bus was comin up the Thruway and how it was all freaks and everyone laughin, singin and passin around dope, and the bus stalled in traffic and the kids saw this cat standin in the road and needin a ride and they all started jumpin up and down and yellin "Pick him up!" "Pick him up!" "Pick him up!" and the bus driver began sweatin all over and shoutin out things about company regulations and other kinds of horse-shit. A sort of instant people's militia was formed and they started up the aisle when all of a sudden the bus doors opened and this freak with a knapsack on his back came aboard. Everybody was jokin and clownin and even the bus driver felt better. He didn't accept the joint a cat tried to lay on him but he scratched the guy's shaggy head of hair and smiled.

I ain't never gonna forget that story, No sir, Flower Power ain't dead at all, brother, all we gotta do is get our shit together, and grow some thorns ... power to the People! Power to the WOODSTOCK NATION!

Selling It Like It Is

Penney paid $3,500 for a two-day crash course attended by seven merchandising executives anxious to learn how to dig kids. The course included speakers (a journalist, a child psychologist, a seventeen-year-old who publishes an underground newspaper) and fieldwork (a visit with a disk jockey, a trip to Marty Limbo's far-out clothing store in New York's East Village, dinner at Max's Kansas City, a light concert at Fillmore East). On finishing up, the Penney executives were handed home-study kits in paper bags colored orange, yellow, purple, and fuchsia. The contents: a kaleidoscope, a water pistol, a yo-yo, a Lotus Land poster of a chocolate-brown nude girl with flowers in her hair, a poster of a nude boy on a blue swan in a purple lake, a long-playing record of the Rascals, a small gold bell, some underground newspapers, an aboveground magazine (Eye) aimed at teen-agers, a package of incense, a stash for marijuana (empty), and a small mirror. Penney is brooding about the implications for its future of a generation that may be growing up disdainful of brand loyalties and store images. The company finds some of the implications distinctly favorable. "We have a square image," says Edward Gorman, assistant to the president and a specialist in merchandising. "But square is in. Honesty is in. Cheap is in. Kids are moving toward a 'tell it like it is' philosophy. I think we can hit them right in the eyes with a 'sell it like it is' approach."

Fortune
January, 1969

Here comes the song the true folks of WOODSTOCK NATION would call a "bummer." Yesterday as I walked into the uptown building to see the publisher a bright red-and-white sign winked out of a glass case in the lobby:

DO YOUR OWN THING
BANK AT CHASE MANHATTAN

Before we return to the glories of the WOODSTOCK NATION we would like to pause for a moment for this important announcement....

The Impact of Youth

By 1970 almost one out of every three persons in the U.S. will be under the age of 25. During the 1970's this youth market will control over $45 billion in spending power annually (and it is growing at a phenomenal rate). Because of this, companies in the 1970's who continue to use today's marketing strategies will almost surely suffer a reduction in market share or, more seriously, total company extinction.... Fads must be pursued, youth buying-behavior must be analyzed... This conference will bring together the largest group of youth-oriented experts ever assembled.

(Promotional brochure — "Selling the American Youth Market," AMR International, Inc.)

Brothers and Sisters, we have a duty to each other to work out the problem of the vultures that prey on our culture and indeed on the rest of the world culture as well. The above quote is advertising a conference on youth to be held in the Waldorf-Astoria, October 20-21, price of admission $300. People attending will hear from such mind-manipulators as Stanton Freeman, president Electric Circuses Discotheques, Russell D. Barnard, Assistant to the Vice President, Marketing, CBS records, and Barbara E. Kelley, Vice President, Director of Advertising, Cole of California. About thirty such "youth experts" will attend and lay down the rap to winning back the kids and winning them back with some of the same groovy techniques as were employed to found the WOODSTOCK NATION. The fat cats coughing up $300 a ticket give off some really good vibes. Real groovy! Here are a few of the 500 companies or so that will attend and an incomplete list of what they'll be about when this fall you hear them say "We're jus doin our thing, baby."

Their Thing

A.T.&T.

About eight years ago A.T.&T. was sued by the government for screwing the American public out of seven billion dollars in phony rate increases. Last year A.T.&T. made a net profit of eight and one-half billion dollars. That's more than the Gross National Product of more than 85 per cent of the nations in the world.

Dow Chemical

Let's hear it for napalm production!

International Harvester

Keeps them sharecroppers down on the farm with exorbitant prices on equipment and deals with large syndicates.

Schick

Sponsor of right-wing campaigns.

U.S. Army

Not to be confused with the Boy Scouts.

Chase Manhattan Bank

Heavy financial support to South Africa.

Anaconda Copper and Aluminum

Owns more of South America than Brazil and Argentina combined.

Bank of America

Chief backer of California grape owners. "Don't Eat Grapes" or for that matter the Bank of America either.

Merck, Sharpe, & Dome

One of the leading supporters of the AMA and lobbyists against free medical care.

Monsanto Chemicals

Try chemical and biological warfare. By the way, did you know that PIG NATION has enough ANTHRAX to destroy the world eighty times over. Thought you'd like to know.

96 So the Big Boys are going to get together and sort

of figure out how they can make some bread on the WOODSTOCK NATION or, if not directly, how they can suck its energy. All that has to be fit in along with Columbia Records pulling ads out of the underground press in an effort to cripple them. A top research firm had suggested two ways to prevent another Chicago from happening.*

1. Cancel the policy of youth fare on airplanes.
2. Urge Columbia Records to pull out of the underground press.

As you can see, these guys ain't schmucks like J. Edgar Hoover and his pack of dumb dinosaurs. These guys were prepared to do anything to stay in business, even grow their hair a little longer and put on some beads.

Fit all that in with Love Food, Inc. selling sawdust burgers for outrageous prices on the highest hill in WOODSTOCK NATION and shoveling real money with real shovels into Wells Fargo Trucks, all the time guarded by cops who weren't holding flowers in their hands, no sir. These are things that weren't announced from the stage in that syrruppy smooth groovyvoice, nor talked about in the psychedelic hand-outs and press releases of Woodstock Ventures. The hope is that PIG NATION cannot endorse what happened up in WOODSTOCK NATION. The hope is that they can never even figure out what happened until it's too late. The hope is that the people will always be stronger than the Pig's technology. The hope is that the Pig is too dumb to dig the scene. That it will continue thinking it was a festival in the making and not the building of a Nation. Can Amerika absorb smoke-ins, fuck-ins, liberated zones, what have you, inside its borders?? I don't think soooo. That's an opinion and not a prediction. No politician can support what went on there, no WOODSTOCK NATION delegate could possibly win a seat in the mother-country Senate or even House for that matter. Only in the eyes of the spaced-out

*Text of report available from the *Ol' Mole,* Boston, Mass.

cynics is this happening. That just ain't what's coming down. Each day in WOODSTOCK NATION there were rumors that Governor Rockefeller (who took that groovy trip to his colonies in South-Amerika last month) was going to declare it as a disaster area. "Disaster" is kind of an interesting word because if you were a revolutionary who thought something heavy was indeed comin down, you were cheering for it to in fact be a disaster for Rockefeller and his whole fuckin world. Disaster is one of those ambiguous terms like a headline up there I saw that said "Chaos Rains" and I wondered why it didn't say "Chaos Reigns" but, well you play those games too don't you? They do on Madison Avenue and they cause a lot of chromosome damage. What if we started playin em and pushin Left Guard instead of Right Guard? But wait....

Fellow revolutionaries of WOODSTOCK NATION and gentlemen of the BOARD OF AMERIKA — here's what *Fortune* Magazine sees when it concludes business's most complete study of the "youthquake":

> At the moment, they seem quite capable of bringing the disorders that have beset the campuses into much of their parents' world — into business and government. We should begin to discern their choice in another year or two. END

Fortune magazine ain't Fortune Cookies! They ain't fucking around. America has fantastic selling capabilities. Nixon's making money on Black Power, everyone's cleaning up on the MOON. "Wonder what the revolutionaries are thinking at United Artists?" says the ad in today's paper. And well, dig, conspiracy time-bomb toys and authentic Yippie love beads and the No. 1 bestselling paperback today is, take it away... ELDRIDGE CLEAVER's *Soul on Ice*. The most brilliant, tough-ass motherfucker around and Hollywood wants the movie rights.

Hope you all have a groovy time figurin this out. Frankly it gives me a headache. It's not without hope though dig. Two of those concession stands at Woodstock got burned to the ground, locals who wanted to make a killing selling apples for fifty cents got ripped off good. Friday night late when the rain came pouring down in buckets kids came running into the woods down "Gentle Way" and "Groovy Lane." They were shivering cold and sneezing. Hip merchants in cute little forest stalls were peddling their wares. Kids asked, "Can we get in there out of this rain?" and a lot said "Sure, come on in, brother!" but some didn't. I saw one glorious rip-off when two Robin Hoods dumped all the hippy junk right into Groovy Lane while another Robin Hood (who was carrying *Revolution for the Hell of It* I'm proud to say) picked his teeth with a knife. All this was happening to the tune of Joan Baez* courageously holding forth in the rainstorm, heavy with child, singing

> Deep in my heart, I do believe,
> We shall overcome someday.

*One of the best bits I pulled was with Baez on Saturday night. We met years ago in Cambridge around the Mount Auburn Coffee House when we both liked motorcycles. By the beginning of WOODSTOCK NATION, I had become very ambiguous about her. I didn't like her form of pacifism as opposed to say Tuli Kupferberg's form with which you could get along — even fall in love. Tuli would respect you even if you walked around with a machine gun. Tuli just liked to have a good time and preaching was a drag. I could never fall in love with Joan Baez, but standing there amidst the amorality of the Rock Empire, with a forty-foot-high, mile-wide light show blazing away, spotlights bouncing off U.S. AIR FORCE Helicopters, and some crazy cat bouncing around in a mechanical swing taking movies of Creedence Clearwater belting it out, well, I felt very close to Joan. We talked about David Harris, her husband in prison, and pacifist Dave Dellinger facing ten years with me for among other bullshit charges "encouraging and teaching the use of incendiary devices." We argued about the way in which people were ripping up draft boards. I said the model of sitting there praying and waiting for the FBI was incorrect. They should just do it over and over again and if they got caught, well that was that, but that waitin stuff was crap. I invited her to see the tree on our roof that Anita and I water each day and then I gave her a beautiful green-and-chrome switchblade and told her to defend herself. "I shall throw it in the river," she sang in her beautiful Mount Carmel voice. And the river sang back, "Use it to slice the morning bread." As I read this it sounds a bit smug; the meeting was more a draw and the knife might have been a gift of love. I've considered that in some of my tender moments I try to hide sometimes, when I write - but not when I make love.

Nightmare or Utopia?

The New York Times Editorial Page 8/18/69

Nightmare in the Catskills

The dreams of marijuana and rock music that drew 300,000 fans and hippies to the Catskills had little more sanity than the impulses that drive the lemmings to march to their deaths in the sea. They ended in a nightmare of mud and stagnation that paralyzed Sullivan County for a whole week-end.

What kind of culture is it that can produce so colossal a mess? One youth dead and at least three others in hospitals from overdoses of drugs; another dead from a mishap while sleeping in an open field. The highways for twenty miles around made completely impassable, not only for the maddened youths but for local residents and ordinary travelers.

Surely the parents, the teachers and indeed all the adults who helped create the society against which these young people are so feverishly rebelling must bear a share of the responsibility for this outrageous episode. It is hardly credible that pot, acid and other illegal drugs could be freely exchanged and used on the scale reported by reliable witnesses.

The sponsors of this event, who apparently had not the slightest concern for the turmoil it would cause, should be made to account for their mismanagement. To try to cram several hundred thousand people into a 600-acre farm with only a few hastily installed sanitary facilities shows a complete lack of responsibility......

As always, there were redeeming features to the generally dismal situation. One was the genuine kindness shown by the residents of Monticello

and other overrun communities, who boiled water and made thousands of sandwiches for the hungry, thirsty hordes of youngsters. Another was the help given by the doctors and nurses who flew to the scene.

Last, but by no means least, was the fact that the great bulk of the freakish-looking intruders behaved astonishingly well, considering the disappointments and discomforts they encountered. They showed that there is real good under their fantastic exteriors, if it can just be aroused to some better purpose than the pursuit of LSD.

CBS Evening News with Walter Cronkite 8/18/69

On the CBS Evening News, commentator John Lawrence stated that what happened at White Lake "may have been more than an uncontrolled outpouring of young people, struggling, as they did, to survive ..." What had happened, he said, was that hundreds of thousands of kids had invaded a resort "totally unprepared to accommodate them," but that somehow "old-fashioned kindness and caring" had brought the young people together "in harmony and good humor" with the inhabitants of the town — "adults who resent and reject their youthful style of life." "All of them learned from the experience," concluded Laurence. "...not that hundreds of thousands of people can paralyze an area and break the law, but that, in an emergency at least, people of all ages are capable of compassion."

Ain't You Glad It's There, Sweetie

In *Revolution for the Hell of It,* lots of karate chops were scored against the midriff of *The New York Times.* It was interesting that my hometown newspaper the *Worcester Telegram and Gazette* panned the book something fierce.* The thing they got really pissed about was my attack on one of "America's most cherished institutions, *The New York Times.*" The *Times* symbolizes everything I hate in PIG NATION. The smugness of having all the news that's fit to print. What arrogance! They have an ad that runs on television (all words, no pictures) that says as it unrolls like some biblical scroll, "Even if you don't read it all it's nice to know it's there." Dig that! The PIG NATION's Security Blanket. Picture all those middle-age executives sucking their thumbs while they cradle the *Times* under their arm on the 5:09 to Babylon. Picture the people out in Southampton letting the Real Estate section and the Sports section deliberately lie around unread. "Even if you don't read it all it's nice to know it's there." Bah-humbug. One way to know about power in Amerika is to begin by asking the question, "Who in Amerika feels it's nice to know it's all there?"

*The Worcester Telegram and Gazette is owned by Robert Stoddard, national secretary of the John Birch Society. He owns about half the town including part of my ol man and some day I'm gonna write about Worcester and Robert Stoddard like how's this for starters. Robert Stoddard attends the most WASP church in the world on the corner of Salisbury and Park. In the chapel there is a huge neon juke box machine and you press the buttons to get a sermon. A-4 Death of a Loved One; B-6 Loss of Property; D-3 Business Difficulties. One night me and this young minister who was active in civil rights and lost his pulpit went in there totally zonked on Colombian Grass and listened to the juke box play sermons for at least an hour as we boogalooed up the aisles.

The Worcester Telegram and the left-wing *Guardian* were the only two bad reviews of *Revolution for the Hell of It.* My favorites were a review in the Kansas State Penitentiary paper called "Stretch" and a letter attacking the favorable review in *Time* magazine. It is an angry right-wingy type letter written by Pat McNeil. In point of fact, I wrote it while I lay in the hospital somewhere in the Bronx. It was also significant that *The New York Times* chose Jack Newfield to review the book and not Richard Goldstein. Newfield is to the political revolution what Goldstein is to the cultural struggle. Maybe you'd be interested in my review of the book? Here's a

Last spring, the day I got busted for conspiracy and later for possession of dangerous weapons, I went to a demonstration against *The New York Times*. It was a left demonstration with lots of correct info about the *Times'* role in the military-industrial complex. I had a shirt that said "I got my job thru Granma" and I made a lot of headway talking to the *Times* truck drivers about how the *Times* had no respect for them and that's why they didn't have any funnies. To show them what I meant I had two toilet paper rolls made up using the N.Y. *Times.* In WOODSTOCK NATION that's all the *Times* is good for and on some psychic level the *Times* understands this and that's why they see it as a Nightmare.

Not so with television, and certainly not so with CBS-TV, the hippest of the big three even if Walter Cronkite made the most sickening apology to Daley I ever heard. Jack Lawrence, who I know well, is very sympathetic to the "Movement" even if he does use phrases like "wide-eyed anarchists looking for trouble." Like almost everyone in the left I have a genuine suspicion of the mass media and especially television. A suspicion which is highly justified. But the trouble is that too paranoid a suspicion leaves you no way to deal with it. It tells you nothing about how television works and sets up a plastic dome where you don't have to think about the impact on our minds of color TV, cable TV and knowing that some day real soon most families in PIG NATION will be able through their TV sets to have a computer at their disposal. It just seems stupid to me how people who want to create a revolution can avoid trying to master the most revolutionary means of communication since language itself was invented. Marxists — run-of-the-mill Marxists anyway — can conveniently blot out the impact of the great leap forward in technology. Check this fact out for example. *Ninety per cent of all scientists who ever lived are still alive today.* Statistics like that are incomprehensible to Marxist

quicky for the morning readers. "Hoffman shows flashes of brilliance and a fantastic amount of energy, but lacks a deep sensuality." Or: "FREE (the pseudonym under which I wrote) is a shaggy-dog story in search of a punch line."

105

theoreticians. They just don't know how to fit them into their plastic dome. Anarchist theoreticians like Murray Bookchin, founder of *Anarchos** and author of *Listen Marxist!*, understand far better the implications of post-scarcity economy. Murray would have understood well the piles of garbage in WOODSTOCK NATION, he would have understood why all the printing press and mimeograph machines broke down in competition with the gigantic triple-instant video projections of Janis Joplin. Murray is really one cat who's got his shit together even if he's awful hard reading. You ought to get a copy of his magazine.

Anyway I wanted to tell you a secret about television, rather than simply make the obvious point that television, like the helicopter, belongs in the future, while newspapers, like automobiles, belong in WOODSTOCK NATION's trash bucket. Here's a secret that might help you use it better if you feel like fighting in the TV jungle and you only got a switchblade and not millions of dollars to pump images through the funnels of Madison Avenue. Many reporters are Yippie agents. I learned this watching hours and hours of straight unedited footage on Chicago, first in the making of the Yippie movie and later in preparation for the conspiracy trial. It began to become apparent that the individual reporter covering the story had a good deal to do with its conceptualization, with the slant the story took.** This

*Anarchos, P.O. Box 466, Peter Stuyvesant Station, New York, N.Y. 10009

**It's almost impossible to do reporting and especially TV reporting without a slant on the story. Some time when you watch television news shows get out a pencil and paper. Mark down the name of each reporter and each news event and give each reporter a "slant rating" of plus or minus. You can work up a very good scoring index taking such factors as "picture editing," "tone of announcer's voice," "news events that surround the spot," and most importantly, "emotion-ladened words." For example, I just saw a news item on 7:00 NBC-TV. It concerned the Mid-East conflict and although it bluffed at being neutral it was clearly following the government line (as it almost invariably does — *always* on international news) of support for Israel. For one thing the footage was shot in Israel which is already a clue. When the Israelis attacked an Arab village they were "commandoes." When the Arabs attacked an Israeli village they were "terrorists." Seems like "Laugh-In" isn't the only thing on TV that is verrrrry interesting.

is particularly true when a voice-over narrative is used, a technique that CBS-TV follows more than the other channels, which prefer to have the anchormen — i.e. Huntley and Brinkley — narrate a lot of the footage. Television reporters are often young, often in the thick of the battle, often sympathize. Not sympathetic like the National Liberation Front is sympathetic, granted, but close enough to lend a hand. And they hate parents or teachers or bosses. Turn on the cameramen! Every organizer should see a film that will be out just when this book appears called "Medium Cool," about a television reporter who covers the Chicago demonstrations. The picture is more interesting in what it attempts to do than what it achieves. The picture is very pro-movement but before I get carried away with the glories of the mass communications industry, let me tell you about the time I called the producers of "Medium Cool" and asked if they would consider doing a benefit for the conspiracy trial, seeing how they were so sympathetic and we were flat broke with a staff that hadn't gotten any money in three weeks.* You know what they decided at Paramount Pictures? ... We were too "controversial."

Take a piece of dark cellophane plastic and cut out the letters BULLSHIT. Paste this over a wide-faced flashlight or a lamp rigging that you can easily make. Always carry such a rigging to movies in which you want to comment on what's on the screen. Power to the People's critics. (Thanks to Jean-Jacques Lebel)

*We still are broke. If you would like to help us out with bread or find out more about what is probably going to be the biggest trial in our history, you can reach us at The Conspiracy, (312) 427-7773. If you call on September 23rd, on the eve of our trial, you can talk to one of the conspirators and get your voice recorded on phones guaranteed tapped by the FBI. Phones they have admitted tapping, and this ain't no paranoid bullshit.

Most Honorable John Mitchell
Chief Butcher
United States of America

Dear Jack

It has been some time since you have indicted me for conspiracy. It was such a nice,
personal, warm letter, I thought it was about
time I sat down and answered you. After all,
this may be my last chance before your asshole
deputy Foran in Chicago sends me up the river
for ten years or so. I just want to know if
you and the other leaders of PIG NATION would
consider meeting to negotiate a ceasefire and
eventual peace treaty with members of WOODSTOCK
NATION. You must understand that this peace
feeler is exploratory and for obvious reasons
should be kept secret. I will do the same with
any responses from you. To begin with, you
should familiarize yourself with the program of
the Berkeley Liberation Front, the platform of
the White Panther Party and the Yippie demands
for a Free Society to get an idea of where our
heads are at. At the first sign of interest in
negotiations from you, we will meet in conference
with large numbers of our brothers and sisters
and hammer out a single set of demands. Let me
briefly spell out a few minimum requirements so
you can get a whiff of what we'll be smoking
when we sit down together.

    1.   Free John Sinclair and all other political
prisoners.

    2.   Get off our Free Land. As a beginning,
end the occupation of New Mexico, Arizona,
Haight-Ashbury, the Lower East Side, Berkeley
including the University of California, Ann

108

Arbor, Michigan, the Boston Common, Ritten-
house Square in Philadelphia, Big Sur, Provincetown, Lincoln Park in Chicago and the
other Woodstock, New York (negotiable). As
you must realize we already have built and defended Bethel, the Capital of our WOODSTOCK
NATION.

3.   We want the right of free passage to
and from different areas of our Nation. We
do not want to be hassled by your Pigs in any
way, shape, or manner. We will submit to your
system of law only if we do injury to one of
your citizens and we expect you to do likewise.

4.   We want you to give us a specified amount
of time on the television airwaves to show various survival information, theatrical events
like mass fuck-ins, and news reports that affect
the political and cultural life of WOODSTOCK
NATION.

5.   Wherever rivers or lakes flow into or
border our two Nations, you pledge to keep
garbage and other shit out of the water. We'll
do likewise. Perhaps we can work something out
jointly in this area after the war is over. We
will refrain from putting LSD in reservoirs that
service both Nations.

6.   You will allow us opportunity to trans-
port all members of our liberated Nation who
might find themselves trapped in your schools,
factories and other penitentiaries. In reci-
procity, we will look for wayward souls who might
have wandered into our area by mistake. We
will encourage the posting of signs such as
''Come home, Cindy'' and ''John we miss you.''

7.   You will convince the Culture-Vultures
who have taken our culture out of the alleys
and parks of our Nation and turned it into
profits to pay $300,000,000 in reparations and
a mutually agreed upom sum to be negotiated
each year.

110

8.   You will provide us with enough arms
o successfully repel any and all invasions
y warring Pig tribes who fail to live by the
reaty.

These eight areas would provide some basis
or discussion. We would also make some sug-
estions about the BLACK NATION and the rest
f what we call the Free World (although I
elieve you call them something else). You,
f course, realize you must negotiate independ-
ntly with them.
Maybe it all sounds like what my ol man used
o call the ''gimme-gimmes,'' but considering
he consequences you are getting off relatively
heap. In fact, dirt cheap! The alter-
ative will be, I'm afraid, the total and
omplete death of Amerika. The land as
ell as the system. There are many of my
rothers and sisters who would even say these
ight demands are not enough. They would say
nat the brain damage your teachers have
aused is in itself punishable by death, to
ay nothing of the rotten food you tried to
oison us with. But, well I don't want to
lip out into flaming rhetoric in a personal
ommunication such as this. Let's just say I
ope to hear from you before the trial starts.
ou can signal your willingness to negotiate
y smoking a joint on television. Labor Day
ill be as good a day as any. We would be
eady to send a negotiation team to a place
e both agree upon within ten days after you
ignal. Until then, power to the people,
nd hope the missus is feeling better.

.S. You will know this letter is authentic
f you soak it in water for ten minutes and
hen drink the cocktail.

to love we must survive
to survive we must fight...

Survival

At the back of *Revolution for the Hell of It* in small print is the most valuable part of the book. "Fuck the System" presents ways in which you can help take a free trip without working. Not working strikes a blow for freedom, as I'm sure we'll all agree. Here's a few more tips. Some of the best ways to steal I know have been working out very well this year. The first involves getting someone a job as a cashier in a large supermarket, a job that is fairly easy to come by. After about two weeks the cashier invites all brothers and sisters to shop for free (by simply forgetting to ring up the total amount). For a while one operation I know was getting about five hundred dollars worth of food each week. I'm sure you know how to work the credit-card swindle and also how to get double your money on travelers' cheques by reporting them 113 stolen? I doubt if you know how to fly from Boston to San Francisco for fourteen dollars and around the world for eighty-eight? I can't tell you here but if I see you and I think you'll use the information well I'll pass it on. Maybe if you come out to Chicago during the trial.

Next I want to clue you in on the U.S. Government Printing Office, Washington. D.C. You can find out just about anything you want from them, especially on Survival.* They also print the best material available on military tactics in revolutionary warfare. The U.S. Army, for example, puts out unquestionably the most important books available on the subject of street fighting and resistance to military (police) repression. Another publication that's probably the most valuable work of its kind available is called *Physical Security* and has more relevant information than Che Guevara's *Guerilla Warfare.* The chapter on Sabotage is extremely precise and accurate with detailed instructions on the making of all sorts of homemade bombs and triggering mechanisms. That information, combined with *Army Installations in the Continental United States* and a lot of guts, can really get something going!

The U.S. Government is an expert on living free and creating destruction; it's been doing both for quite a long time. I ain't saying you should use any of this information, in fact for the records of the FBI, I say right now "Don't blow up your local draft board or other such holy places." You wouldn't want to get the Government Printing Office indicted for conspiracy, would you now?

---

*Some of the best tools of Survival are available in the most fantastic development in its field — *The Whole Earth Catalogue,* Portola Institute, 558 Santa Cruz Avenue, Menlo Park, California, 94025. GET IT!

c. Other simple incendiary devices can be made of mixtures of gasoline and oil, or thickened fuel, rigged to be fired by a time fuse or by electrical or mechanical igniters.

24. Disguised Incendiary Devices

Since the entire incendiary device is actually an initiator and depends on a combustible target for its effect it can be made small in size. This small size permits an incendiary device to be disguised as a commonplace item. Manufactured incendiary devices have been concealed in cakes of soap, pieces of imitation coal, cigarette packs, pencils and fountain pens (fig. 2). Even undisguised items, because of their size and their natural appearance as a component of some larger mechanism, do not attract particular attention. Chemical and clockwork contrivances are among the latter types.

25. Mechanical Delay Devices

Mechanical delay devices are used normally in connection with dry cell electric batteries. The basic idea in these mechanisms can be well represented by the use of an ordinary pocket

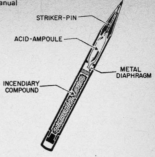

Figure 2. Disguised incendiary device (mechanical pencil).

watch. By removing the minute hand, setting a small screw in the crystal to a depth that it will contact the hour hand but not the watch face, and using this screw and the main stem as contact point, the watch becomes a timing delay mechanism with a 12-hour span. This same

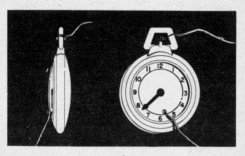

Figure 3. Improvised mechanical delay device (pocket watch).

STEEL PIPE
FILLED WITH
EXPLOSIVE

—FUSE

NOTE: *IN THIS TYPE OF BOMB A
DETONATOR MAY BE AFFIXED TO
THE FUSE IF THE EXPLOSIVE
CHARGE IS A HIGH EXPLOSIVE, BUT
IS NOT USED WHEN THE CHARGE
IS A LOW EXPLOSIVE.*

Figure 5. Steel pipe filled with explosives.

MAGNETIC CLAM

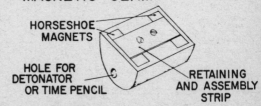

HORSESHOE
MAGNETS

HOLE FOR
DETONATOR
OR TIME PENCIL

RETAINING
AND ASSEMBLY
STRIP

NOTE: *THIS BOMB IS MADE OF THE GERMAN
SABOTAGE EXPLOSIVE NIPOLIT. THE HARD CAST,
SOAPSTONE-LIKE EXPLOSIVE MATERIAL IS HOLLOWED
OUT TO RECEIVE THE HORSESHOE MAGNETS. IT HAS
A HOLE BORED IN ONE END TO RECEIVE A
DETONATOR OR TIME PENCIL. IN SOME CASES THE
RETAINING STRIP MAY BE COLORED RED.*

Figure 4. Magnetic clam.

Figure 1. Improvised incendiary delay device.

Down On Me and Janis Joplin

God, I'd like to fuck Janis Joplin!

Down on me, down on me,
Looks like ev'rybody in this whole round world
Is down on me.

Love in this world is so hard to find,
When you've got yours and I've got mine.
That's why it looks like ev'rybody in this
    whole round world

Is down on me.

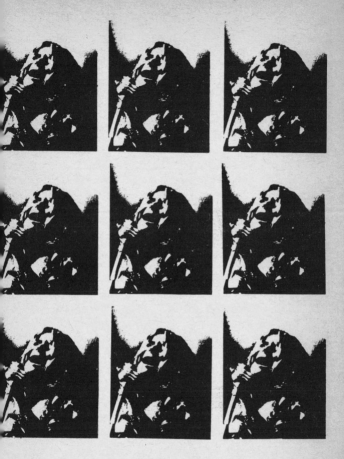

Man, I just love her belting out heavy little-girl truck-driver blues. Love her swingin her Southern Comfort ass and choking the mike. Love her outa sight costumes and the way she swaggers around like Annie Oakley from the Wild West Show. She's Ma Baker and Baby Snooks. She's out of her fuckin mind Janis is ... when she sings you hear the sadness of Billie Holliday and Bessie Smith the way they got their lives into their sound. Janis can do it. Janis sings the same song over and over again. Gooooo down on me ... and I don't feel cheated one bit when I hear her sing it cause it's a great fuckin song and Janis is all fuckin right even if she don't know from California grapes and freeing John Sinclair ... maybe it ain't her fault? Maybe it's mine??? Maybe I ain't explained it to her right?? Those rock folks are into something and loving Janis is a way of saying I'm sorry if I'm really fuckin up your scene. I think you folks are into something really beautiful and really heavy, even — and let me say it loud and clear; even *The Who* is GREAT. You cats got some good shit goin, like the Dead doing freebees in the park and Gracie Slick saying "motherfucker" on the Dick Cavett Show. Dig that PIG NATION, "motherfucker"! Wait til you hear the Jefferson Airplane's next album *"Volunteers of America."*

Tear down the walls
Tear down the walls

Come on now together
Get it on together
Everybody together

If you get into digging the music it's all "tear down the walls, motherfucker" and "kick out the jams, 'motherfucker.' " It's Janis saying loud and clear, right on the stage of WOODSTOCK NATION:

Don't take no shit from nobody ...
Tell em all to fuck off.

It's the Doors' warning in "When the Music's Over" —
"We want the world and we want it NOW!"

That's good enough politics for me ... Hard on, sister! Lay it on em, brother! Sure it'd be nice if Sly and the Family Stone stopped playing once and looked out at PIG NATION and said "Oh, by the way we're Communists," God that would blow a lot of fuckin holes in "His Master's Voice." Yeh, but maybe that's unfair cause on the other hand we politicos don't sing too good. When SDS talks about the Vanguard they don't mean the record company, but they don't mean fuckin and dancin with all the people either. They mean responsible leadership just the way my father does. And what about bands like The Who??? Heroes of the people; do they have responsibilities? What are you gonna do with your bread, brother rock stars? Are you gonna help build and defend the WOODSTOCK NATION NOW, or are you just gonna piss it all away?? Here's a word of advice from one of the biggest dudes around. His name is Chairman Mao. He and his rock band built a whole fuckin Nation of 700,000,000 people when they said it couldn't be done. This quote is for me as much as you cause when I get through with this book I'm gonna learn how to sing....

> You have many good qualities and have rendered great service, but you must always remember not to become conceited. You are respected by all, and quite rightly, but this easily leads to conceit. If you become conceited, if you are not modest and cease to exert yourselves, and if you do not respect others, do not respect the cadres and the masses, then you will cease to be heroes and models. There have been such people in the past, and I hope you will not follow their example.

> "We Must Learn to Do Economic Work" (January 10, 1945) *Selected Works*, Vol. III, p. 239.

The Beatles may be more popular than Jesus but heavy cats like Chairman Mao, Uncle Ho, and beautiful long-haired Che Guevara are more popular than even the Beatles. You ought to check out that other "free world" and see. Don't take my word for it — but don't believe *Variety* or *Billboard* or even *Rolling Stone* either. Any of you guys want to play in Havana Square for free just get in touch. We've already made the arrangements.

LONG LIVE THE CULTURAL REVOLUTION!   121

Talk-ROCK

THE WHO vs. THE WHAT in the Battle of the BANDS

WE'RE NOT GONNA TAKE IT!*	WE'RE GONNA TAKE IT!**

WE'RE NOT GONNA TAKE IT!*

Welcome to the camp
I guess you all know why we're here.
My name is Tommy and I became
   aware this year

If you want to follow me
You've got to play pinball.
So put in your ear plugs
Put on your shades
And you know where to put
   the cork!

Hey you gettin drunk
So sorry, I've got you sussed
Hey you smokin mother nature,
This is a bust,
Hey hung up old mister normal
Don't try to gain my trust.
Cos you ain't gonna follow me
Any of those ways
Although you think you must!

We're not gonna take it.
We're not gonna take it.
We're not gonna take it,
Never did and never will,
We're not gonna take it
Gonna break it!

WE'RE GONNA TAKE IT!**

Chicago? People's Park?
   Free Rock? What happened,
   Who?
Peter, how can we follow you
when you admire Hitler?
Hitler?
Hitler?
You mean stick it up whose
   ass, Who? Whose ass?
   Nixon's ass? Huh, Who?

Yeah we sure is stoned.

That's good baby.

What about when you said
   you worn your hair long
   for business?
Anyway! Do--wa--do--wa.
   You Must!

We're gonna take it.
We're gonna take it.
We're gonna take it.

Outa sight!

*From the long-playing album "Tommy."
**From the short-playing album "Tommy-Gun."

<table>
<tr><td>

Gonna shake it!
Let's forget it better still!

Now you can hear me,
Your ears are truly sealed.
You can't speak either,
Your mouth is filled.
You can't see nothing
And pin ball completes the scene.
Here comes Uncle Ernie
To guide you to
Your very own machine.

We're not gonna take it!
We're not gonna take it!
We're not gonna take it,
Never did and never will
Don't want no religion
And as far as we can tell
We ain't gonna take you

Never did and never will

We're not gonna take you!
We forsake you!
Gonna rape you!
Let's forget you better still!
Let's forget you better still!

We forsake you

Gonna rape you
Let's forget you ... better still!

124

</td><td>

Fuckin All right!
Why should we forget ... we
    love to fuck and make
    revolution.
How can we hear you ...
The cash register is so loud ...
Filled with Yankee Bread ...
Give your bread away and see ...

That's cute ... la de da.

Machine guns, Who ... we
    need machine guns!

We're gonna take it.
We're gonna take it.
We're gonna take it.

Fuck the Pope!
Fuck the Nuns!
So how come your manager
    demanded $11,500 before
    you went on the stage Who??
    Couldn't you wait an hour to
    get paid? Who?
Bullshit!
Bullshit!
Rape! I thought this was
    peace and music Who?
Who are you Who ——
    Who are you Who ——
    You Whooo-Who-are-you
How can we forsake John
    Sinclair?
Rape you! Who
Un-unh we ain't gonna for-
    get Big John. Ten years
    for two joints — Who

</td></tr>
</table>

See me ...	How can we see you Who you're at the Concord Hotel with my ol man?
Feel me ...	How can we feel you Who the stage is twenty feet high?
Touch me ...	How can we touch you Who you're in the helicopters, way up there ...
Heal me ...	Who you don't even know where the hospital is Who?
See me ...	Where's your money goin Who?
Feel me ...	What about John Sinclair Who?
Touch me ...	Who you're in Grossinger's with my ol man Who?
Heal me ...	Who why don't you come up to the Hospital and sing for the troops Who?
Listening to you I get the music.	The money is the message Who?
Gazing at you I get the heat	
Following you I climb the mountain	Following Who Who?
I get excitement at your feet!	
Right behind you I see the millions	You see millions Who? But you don't see John Sinclair. Where's John Who? There are millions in prison Who? You-Who-You-Who —
On you I see the glory.	
From you I get opinions	See you later Who baby, I climb my own mountain ——
From you I get the story	See if you can help out the people who's gettin busted who ——'preciate it Who-ooooooooo. So long ....

"Wonder who that Masked Bandit was? All he left was
two silver joints?" –
"I don't know, some people call him the WHAT ..."
Hi yo WHOOOOOO
You feel all right kimusavi?
No faithful hippie companion – I had one too many
blues –

125

The Great Rip-Off

Ring ... Ring ... Ring Hello Woodstock Ventures
... Is Michael Lang there, George Metesky the
Deputy of Defense for the Youth International
Party – you know, the Yippies that put on the
festival in Chicago last year ... that's right,
Abbie Hoffman, Minister of Culture for the
Yippies and representatives from other move-
ment groups would like to see Mr. Lang about
the festival.

I'm not sure you'd want to, this is going to be
three days of Peace and Music, it's not about
politics ...

Oh yes, well neither are the Yippies, we just
want to dig on the groovy doovy vibes. Tell Mr.
Lang we'll be at his office at eleven a.m. tomorrow ... see you then ... CLICK.

The wheels had been set in motion. Everyone was
ready for the pressure treatment ... jamming switchboards, blocking their offices, press conferences
announcing that the crazy communists who ripped up
Chicago were hoping the town board members of
Bethel would give Woodstock Ventures a permit so
we could come up and screw all their daughters —
etcetera, etcetera.

Every group was broke cause the liberal bulge that
used to support most radical causes was off on some
other trip, playing around with anti-ABM campaigns
and sending food to Biafra. Even though they wept
and shed some blood in the streets of Chicago, they
were gone for good — gone with their money. Our
revolution was becoming too radical or crazy or
violent or young. We were fuckin up their cocktail
parties and it mattered not the blood we were shedding or the growing fascism in the country. New ways
had to be found to get bread cause the days of the
mailings and benefits were over. In fact, for the
Yippies, they had never even begun. For six weeks I
had been working on the Movement Speakers' Bureau
project designed to get speakers on the campuses and
have the agency fees available to groups that the

*Movement Speakers' Bureau, 333 East 5th Street, New
York, N.Y. 10003. Send for a free catalogue if you can help
out.

speakers wanted to support. If campus activists put a lot of James Forman-type pressure on filthy-rich student councils, the project could realize a lot of bread. Revolution was becoming a saleable commodity and the only way to deal with that was to try and rip off the bread and spread it around like the manure it was. Besides it was a "safe" project and would keep me off the streets for a while, hence out of jail. I was tired of getting arrested and had even considered cutting my hair and leaving New York. It was a depressing summer of sitting in courtrooms and waiting for the Big Trial to begin in Chicago. I found I spent a lot of time discussing my arrests and wondering if I would end up like Lenny Bruce. The picture of him lying naked on the bathroom floor that I had seen flashed through my mind each day. The Lower East Side was disappearing out of my plastic dome. I was sick of starting free stores that ended up garbage cans, and bailing out people who never gave the bread back so we would get others out, and mimeos that broke down. I wasn't the only one getting sick of New York; even the gutsy Motherfuckers had split to New Mexico, Massachusetts and San Francisco. The bikers were shooting each other in the streets and the drug scene was all speed. Cops stopped cars illegally and threw people against walls and somehow nobody gave a shit because the whole scene had been wasted. Jerry Rubin was in retreat completing his book ... SDS was interested in having Yippies play a role in their fall demonstrations but when they said it was for those who missed Chicago last year most of us lost interest seeing as how we had been there. A lot of my friends were in jail for dope with high or no bail and you couldn't do much about it. One I felt almost responsible for and can't even talk about cause if the FBI found out we were working together, he would be worse off than he already is. I even have to write him under another name. The paranoids were out in force. If a group got something really heavy together it couldn't even talk about it cause everything was tapped and every other guy was a cop.

It's in those moments that you start to think about being white and male and over thirty and too smart for your own fuckin good. You start to get pretty

127

down in the dumps sometimes. Besides, every group was into calling the other an imposter and fights were breaking out all over the place. The left was moving into Stalinism and the hippies were moving to the country (as usual). It was getting mighty lonely on the fence. So there I was organizing left-movement groups to go to a hip community event ... the Morea-Eel of the Motherfuckers, whose role I sometimes think is just to chew me out, would be pissed but it was impossible to contact him. Besides he was always pissed and would be even if he got a cut of the bread. Even if he got a cut of the bread from this book he'd be pissed. Everything had to happen fast too, since Woodstock Ventures' permit hassles would soon be over and they would be less likely to give in. Besides, the festival was only two weeks away. Asking that people should get in free would be ridiculous cause the word was already out about Los Angeles, Denver, and Newport. Tear down the walls and you get in free. Everybody was hip to free and walls were coming down everywhere, but we were into something else. There's a word for it but we'll avoid its usage for various legal reasons. We wanted support from the hip profiteers and we wanted to establish a model for movement groups around the country on how to relate to these huge gatherings. No real hip activist could just sit by and watch skilled promoters create events that gathered huge numbers of young people and made exorbitant profits without eventually taking an interest.

When the twelve of us barged into the Woodstock Ventures offices with police dogs and theatre prop chains hanging out of our pockets we were looking for some bread clear and simple. The mini-skirts flew in all directions and I wondered which one was the gal who said "We're not into politics." We did our little song-and-dance number and said, "We'll be back tomorrow and the fuckers running the show better be

---

*One good way to protect the security of your gang is to all turn on together with LSD. A cop would smoke pot but he sure as hell would never drop acid. Also I've never seen an undercover cop with real long hair and I've seen a lot of undercover cops. Maybe long side-burns and a coupla day's growth of beard, but no Pig is gonna go home to Queens each night or on weekends and play golf with his buddies lookin like Tiny Tim. Ah you kiddin?

here cause there isn't much time — Wa-do-wa- Wa-do-wa." In five minutes we were out and back on the streets of the Lower East Side. Meanwhile, reports kept coming in about who made decisions in their organization and who we should insist should be at that meeting. The call came an hour later from Bethel. They would meet with us tomorrow any place we liked and all four were coming. When they said all four were coming we already had a sense of victory and the opening figure doubled.* There were also people within their organization who for one reason or another were angry, and all day they kept feeding us information about decisions. Their organization was as sloppy as their offices, or ours for that matter. By the time we sat down the next day everything had already been decided and we just had to play out our respective roles and then get stoned together. Up to then, me and Peter, a cat who was in "Movers and Things," a sort of hip cooperative employment agency, were more or less making decisions. Peter was unpopular among lots of groups, but so was I for that matter, or anybody. This was not quite the summer of love and even though the word "community" was thrown around, so were fists and chains.

For the second encounter, Jeff Shero came aboard. Jeff is editor of the *Rat*, probably, with the exception of the *Berkeley Tribe*, the most influential underground paper.** Well, that is, I suppose, if your conception of the underground is what culminates in actions like Chicago and People's Park. The *Rat* brought the underground press to Chicago and was instrumental in organizing high school kids in New York. At the media conference the *Rat* led the difficult struggle for unity and militancy. The *Rat* had tried best of all to relate to the politics of hip from an organizing point of view. I recognized this and I also recognized that Jeff didn't like me much. It was awkward cause I dug him. When he attacked a wild, at times dumb article I wrote on SDS, I even an-

*Actually only three showed up. Roberts stayed uptown to guard the checkbook.

**A month before this meeting the staff of the *Berkeley Barb* revolted and began publishing their own paper. It was a ringing lesson to hip capitalists, and in the East we carefully watched and waited to see who would be next.

swered with a letter. It was the first time I had answered criticism in print in seven years — a record I had been rather proud of. Now I wasn't proud of the attack on SDS or the answering of Jeff's criticism. Our relationship was a mess. Still, Jeff sensed my isolation and knew the difficulties we were having getting interest in the conspiracy trial and I knew the *Rat*, like the other underground papers, was feeling the squeeze of the new sex-ploitation mags that were crowding them off the newsstands. In fact, I had heard that the *Rat* was about to fold. All this brought us together and when Jeff, who is Alice's man, said, "Alice says I have a tendency to snub you," I knew we could work together. So it was good to see Jeff involved; besides, Jeff had opened negotiations on a separate front with them and had already met with them. Now there were about a dozen groups represented.

After about an hour of us yelling "Culture-Vultures!" — and them saying "Groovy baby, we dig you guys and your whole scene" we reached an agreement: ten grand, a few hundred tickets, booth space and mutual cooperation on doctors, lawyers and a bail fund for people who would get busted on the way up. We told them up front that we were still into urging people to go free. There were promises of more to come if they made bread on the event. There were a lot of promises.

Who got money? How were we now going to relate to the festival? How were we going to make decisions? There were still going to be problems, especially once other groups found out about the rip-off. It never ceased to amaze me how groups, instead of imitating our model and trying to rip off Woodstock Ventures again or the Fillmore or Columbia Records, tried instead to devour us. Maybe it's just that money sucks. Who knows? I know one thing though, that the little asshole-pseudo-revolutionary gang that tried to rip me off with the same guerilla chain-theatre bit is never gonna get shit. Ripping off guys who just got ten grand for projects and were prepared to fuck up some offices and go to jail, when three blocks away the fat cats are rolling up a two-million-dollar budget, ain't good revolutionary strategy ... but then again, bad tactics were never at a loss in the movement, and especially not in the New York movement. It always puzzled me why the good guys always were the pacifists.

So a lot of meetings happened, and things were pulled together; mimeos, doctors, lawyers, theatre groups, a huge new Trojan Horse of a press, silk-screening operations with some beautiful posters like one that said, "When Tyranny is Law, Revolution is Order." Everyone was rushing to get it all together, too fast in a way, because we weren't sure we knew what the fuck we were doing. People were scared of gettin "CO-OPTED," which on the left is like halitosis or some other catastrophe.* Larry from *Newsreel* coined the term "Vanguard Capitalism" to describe the producers, and that helped a little, but we were sinking in the marshmallow of tolerance and everyone knew it. The night Hugh Romney of the Hogfarm showed up and said, "We'll be givin out a lot of free food, our chicks will be doin some cookin," everyone booed with glee cause at last everybody had what politicos would call a "bummer" if they spoke that language. Women's Liberation was very big this year, especially at meetings that were mostly male, and especially when it came time to do the cooking, clean up, or fuck.

The Hogfarm played a strange role in the whole caper. Under Vanguard Capitalism the Hogfarmers with their "cool out the tension, build up the good vibes" approach played the role of the cops. It was no secret to everyone that the Hogfarm had been invited to participate to the tune of about six grand with another sixteen grand spent on flying them in from New Mexico along with twenty Indians in a chartered plane. Everyone knew if a fence were to be ripped down or a food stand ripped off or some equipment "borrowed" it would be the Hofgarmers that would stop it, not the hogs or Pigs or cops or whatever you called them. The day before that meeting, four of us went up to Bethel to check out the site and were met by a Hogfarmer who said, "My role is to cool you

*co-opt (koópt), v.t. — co'-op-ted. As used in the sense of being lured to your doom by the power structure. For instance, "Abbie has been co-opted by those uptown mind-controlling Pigs at Random House."

guys out." We had a long rap drivin around those hills about whether he thought there was such a thing as a "good" millionaire if he kept his money and stuff like that. "Hey man," a lefty might have said, "haven't you read Jerome Skulnick on institutional violence?" But seeing as how I'm not a lefty and hadn't read it either, I kept my mouth shut. The Hogfarm's specialty was called "Pudding" — a mass of people-jelly, generally naked, generally fucking or sucking, always giggling and always covered in something like jello or whipped cream or pudding. It's pretty hard to argue with Pudding and besides if you were hungry enough you ate it if you had any brains.

Hugh and I are good friends, lovers really. We work hard, have fun and try to work our thing out the best way we know how with a certain amount of respect for each other. In that meeting with the political groups my closest friend was Hugh. We had known each other the longest. I visited him in the hospital in Pennsylvania when he busted his back trying to crank up one of their crazy buses. I held my aching head when he told me the Hogfarm wanted to try and turn on Mississippi. I liked him even though he ran up a huge phone bill in our office when we had no bread. I liked him even though his 500-pound pig mascot ate the shower curtain and some of an article I was writing when we stored him in our 300-pound office. I liked him and his ol lady Bonnie about as much as you can like people these days. Liking him and diggin his politics was QUITE another story, and conflicts between friendships and politics are something I hope to solve this year, but then again I hoped to solve it last year and on back to when I was born I guess. Anyway, Hogfarm politics proved stronger magic than Movement City's and it wasn't just that the name Movement City stunk, it was that the Hog-farm's politics are survival, and when 300,000 people that you are trying to reach get drenched in a huge rainstorm on some foreign hills, survival is what poli-tics is about. Survival needs first, conversion to revolutionary politics second. *The Needs of the Peo-ple Must Be Met.*

After the rains came, the Hogfarm went right on serving their free food and enjoying themselves, and the lefties, not all the lefties but enough to say it, packed up their leaflets or abandoned them and headed out of WOODSTOCK NATION still thinking it was a festival, or worse, a concentration camp. Those that stayed are better for it all, including me. When you learn to survive in a hostile environment, be it the tear gas parks of Chicago or the mud slopes of WOODSTOCK NATION, you learn a little more of the universal puzzle, you learn a little more about yourself, and you learn about the absurdity of any analysis at all. It's only when you get to the End of Reason can you begin to enter WOODSTOCK NATION. It's only when you cease to have any motives at all can you comprehend the magnitude of the event. It's only then that you can start to enjoy it all. This came to me one night while Paul, Roz and I walked through the darkened "Forest of the Crafts People and Hip Merchants" that separated the Hog-farm site from the main performance area.*   We felt our way along the secret paths for hours — bumping into trees and groping around tents. After getting totally exhausted, we emerged in a lighted area and rushed forward sensing our victory over the maze-like forest. Much to our surprise, we were right back where we started — back among the plywood booths of Movement City, right back in the tents of the Hogfarm. God, I'll tell you something I learned up there in WOODSTOCK NATION — nobody knew where the fuck anything was, not even WOODSTOCK NATION. Like Pete Seeger said, "If you were gonna join it, you had to join it by yourself." Figuring out how to get in and out of the whole thing was a prob-lem as old as Western Civilization and as modern as the traffic jam scenes in Jean Luc-Godard's "Week-end." You entered at the End of Reason, of that I was sure. At least I was consistently sure of that. Which is not bad considered I ain't sure of anything else about that mind blower. I ain't sure of nothing at all.

---

*That the Hogfarm-Movement City battle was no contest at all was proven in the naming of the site, even the politicos even-tually called it the Hogfarm site.

The Sinclair Hospital

The morning after the rains came was the most chaotic sight you could ever imagine. It reminded me of when we had a tornado up in Worcester in 1953. WOODSTOCK NATION was all a wreck, everyone sort of sniffling and sad, when a cat came out of his tent and made a fist at the sky: "Fuck off rain, we're staying here forever!" It was then that the battle began for me. It was then that I felt at peace. It was about 5:00 A.M. and I had a hunk of brown canvas over me with a hole cut out for the head. I reminded myself of General George Patton inspecting the troops in Normandy as I walked around assessing the damage. The main performance area had turned into

a huge slide of mud, people, collapsed tents, over-
turned motorcyles, cans, bottles and GARBAGE
GALORE — man, there was more fuckin garbage
unloaded in WOODSTOCK NATION that night than
in the Lower East Side during the entire garbage
strike. The First Aid Center in the Hogfarm was already crowded and the doctor, a woman volunteer
whom I recognized from Chicago, said the twenty to
thirty doctors the Medical Committee for Human
Rights was flying in at noon were not barely enough.
She and I headed for the First Aid Center close to the
performing area, talking all the way about what had
to be done. I was chewing up the information as fast
as I could cause I had just appointed myself Superin-
tendent of Sinclair Hospital.* I was digesting I.V.
solutions, sutures, gauze pads, salt tablets, penicillin,
Ace bandages, cots, operating rooms, the whole bit. I
was trying to recall everything I knew from my youth
about hospitals and medical supplies. If you want to
know the truth it wasn't such a feat. My ol man owns
a medical supply company and I used to spend time
working there or poking around, depending on
whether it was me or my old man you talked to. Hell,
John would sure be proud of me now; after all those
years of being away from the business and after all
those years of revolution and heart attacks — after all
that, I was finally settling in the Hospital Business. I
was finally coming home to work in the store.
We took over a pink-and-white tent that had been
used to feed the staff and divided it in two sections.
Food section to the left, hospital to the right. Plywood sheets were thrown on the ground and cots
began to be set up. Lee Penn, fresh after beating a
ten-year rap in Chicago, and some guys began paint-
ing huge crosses on sheets using red paint and a hunk

*I didn't think to name it that until it was too late. But I'm
just employing the same historical license that other his-
torians use — namely to fill in with a little bullshit. Naming
things right is very important. Don't forget that!

of Kotex. Another tent was "borrowed" and somebody knocked down the press tent and brought it over to be our BAD TRIP center. We also hustled walkie talkies, chairs, supplies, tables, towels, sheets, ambulances, stretchers. Ron Kaufman, who pulled me outa Chicago and was helping do the Movement Speakers' Bureau got out our electric bullhorn and went into action. Signs went up fast: CUTS, WAITING ROOM, ADMISSION, VOLUNTEERS, REST, EMERGENCY, HEAT TABLETS. Old friends began coming over. Abe Peck, ex-editor of the *Chicago Seed* and one of the best cats alive ran the volunteer operation.* Roy Payne from *Newsreel* took over Information Control and kept the visitors out of the area. New people showed up. Like a really cool-headed gal named Jill who had been an Army supply nurse. She took over the supply coordination which was a huge problem seeing as how we didn't have any. Doctors like Sid and Jeff and more pitched in. A local resident named George headed up the coordination of the ambulances that kept showing up. He came for an hour and stayed twenty-four. Hugh Romney and Bonnie Beautiful, ex-Playboy Bunny, got the whole bum-trip scene together. Sorry if I left some folks out. It was the acid and I ain't slept much since that night. Everyone had a name like William Head Doctor, Sid Cuts, Lee Heat Tablets or Lynn Walkie Talkie. What the fuck's a name anyway. It was amazing to see that whole thing take shape. There were things that tore my brains out like dig this: We were centered right next to the helicopter field and helicopters kept flying overhead pulling up the hospital tents. Trying to keep them away was an almost useless task cause there were about five different

---

*To show you how fucked up things are in PIG NATION the grand jury that indicted us in Chicago questioned Abe for two hours about a plot Jerry and I had supposedly cooked up to assassinate Abe!

chains of command working with those helicopters. I mean, after all, this was show business and the show must go on so tents were uprooted and amplifiers battled with stretchers and rock stars with doctors and even champagne with intravenous solutions. In the end the show people won out over the hospital people and medical supplies had to be flown in by none other than — take it away — the United States Air Force!

> Sir, where do I put these supplies, sir. I
> was told to bring these to you. I'm Captain
> Grant of the U.S. Air Force ...

It was just about then that I decided to drop the second of the acid tabs people had been laying on me. It was either the blue or the green ... There we were with helicopters making winds up to thirty or forty miles an hour buzzing around like flies, staring across Lake Shore Drive at a People Hill that was now at least 300,000 strong, listening to what sounded like wildman Joe Cocker, beltin it out from the stage. There we were; Aldo Ray from "Battle Cry" and Dennis Hopper from "Easy Rider" one just back from Nam and the other from Lincoln Park. There we were together luggin boxes of medical supplies into the Sinclair Hospital. "Hey Captain, you ever consider defecting?" I whispered in his ear.

It was about then I took a break and tried to meet a girl or two and feel the acid melt my mind and maybe even hear some sounds. Maybe I could even hustle up some bread for ol John or ol Conspiracy or any ol politics and feel right about members of the Woodstock Four slappin me on the back and treating me like one of the partners... Everything was sort of floating along like this when the first major crack occurred in my plastic dome which by now was beginning to feel sort of mescaline-mellow. A few fireworks were bursting over at People Hill and in my dome, sparklers were starting to light up, too....first white....then green....then rainbow!

Bad Acid

There were bad trips happening all day. Nothing really heavy. Nothing the Hogfarm couldn't handle. You never really knew what caused bad trips and you were sure nobody else who knew anything about acid knew either. You knew about the sugar and orange juice cure and Niacinamide tablets and Thorazine suppositories up the ass and when, as a last resort, to call a doctor. You even knew the most important way to bring someone down was sympathetic kind talk by someone who had been there. Even knowing all that you still didn't know what caused bad trips. Was it strychnine or loss of ego? Was it belladonna or the urban crisis? Was it no food and water or the loneliness of being in a crowd of 300,000? One thing I knew for sure, though, was that announcements like "The blue acid is real bad — report to the hospital if you feel sick," and "The greens are poison"* didn't help one bit, no sir, not one bit. Especially when they were coming out of those microphones that everyone had plugged into their skulls. Those announcements blew fuses in a lot of plastic domes. Hugh, Abe, and I

---

*I only heard this one was announced. Rumors were flying like crazy that night. More people got killed and got born than were even there. People saw more things in the woods and in the sky than on the stage. It was the land of the Heebiejeebies all right and all the witches came out to play.

stood at the admission gate trying to joke with the Mob of Bad Trippers ... like about two hundred were into fits and more were pouring down the road like some mighty St. Vitus Dance all jerking around in their own insanities, sometimes six or eight people carrying some vibrating freak. "It's okay," I said to one cat: "Look, it ain't bad," and I popped in the last tab I had — either the red Abe gave me or the blue or ... gee those sparklers were sure lighting up the sky I noticed, and the bonfires and waterfalls up there weren't bad either.

Hugh and I decided to head for the stage to announce

or Bad Announcements?

that it wasn't bad acid after all!!! It was just as we were working our way across this wobbly bridge that connected performers, helicopters and hospital to stage, microphones and People Hill, that I started to get some doubts ... Things were becoming very unclear and when I saw a guy throw a spear at me like in the movie "Bwana Devil" and I even saw the red-and-green tint that you saw when your 3D glasses fell off, when I saw that, and when I ducked no less, I knew I was on some real powerful shit. I knew I had taken some weird acid ... the trouble was I couldn't figure out whether it was the red or the green, or the blue or the no sleep or the 360,000 people, or the shaky bridge, or that African spear thrower.

The Battle of the MICS *

Just before I climbed down the stairs on the other side of LSD Drive, I remember taking the name tag off my shirt that said GENERAL COORDINATOR. General Coordinator was something I made up to get me past ushers, especially the pushy ones in the green jackets. I have no idea how long I was zonked out or what really happened. I recall trying to steal a lot of heavy movie equipment from this trailer, with some mad revolutionary outlaw freaks that shall go unnamed in case some shit is missing. I remember seeing Hugh chasing some guy with a gun who was trying to rob some TV people, or at least Hugh said it was a gun. Mike Lang later said it was a knife and the guy was trying to grab this chick's wallet ... I was climbing along under the stage area ankle-deep in the mud when I looked to my right and then I saw it ... vague at first and then more visible ... holy shit what a fuckin sight! There they were — a girl and a guy

---

*For those of you who ain't into acid, or LSD as you would call it, it is measured in micrograms or mics for short. You can also assume I mean MIKE LANG and MIC-rophones. All I know is that anyway you slice it there were a lot of mics involved.

fuckin away. The girl was a weird-looking blond chick with a big belly, no, she was pregnant, but that ain't all she was ... she had cuts all over her body and her left tit was ... holy shit it wasn't ... Sharon Tate!!!! Oh fuck what's going on??? There humping her from behind ... I'm gonna pass out ... Elvis Presley!!! At least I think it was him cause it was just the bottom half of a naked dude ... all he had on were some blue suede shoes ... man, my mouth was all dry and I ran up on the stage ... there was Mike Lang ... and all of a sudden we were off exploring each other's plastic domes and talking about big things like Empires and little things like cut feet. I kept wonderin how Elvis was makin out ...

"Hey, Mike I saw Elvis, here, how bout that. Elvis came, well most of him anyways."

"Dylan's comin," said Lang.

"Ah you're full of shit," I said, "he's gonna be in England tonight, don't pull that shit on me."

"Nah I ain't kiddin, Abby-baby, he called up and said he might come ..."

"You think he'd dig runnin for president?"

"Nah, that ain't his trip, he's into something else."

"You met him, Mike? What's he into?"

"I don't know for sure but it ain't exactly politics. You ever met him?"

"Yeah, once about seven years ago in Gertie's Folk City down in the West Village. I was trying to get him to do a benefit for civil rights or something ... hey Mike will you introduce us? I sure would like to meet Dylan ... I only know about meetin him through Happy Traum ..."

"There's an easier way ... Abbs ... I'll introduce you. In fact he wants to meet you ..."

"Hey Mike, what about John Sinclair ..."

"No, not that again, Abby-baby ..."

"Yeah, no shit Mike, that's more important than even Dylan for President ... We ought to get John Sinclair out of jail. He got ten fuckin years for two joints ... 141

how can we take such shit?

"Yeah, that sure was a bummer ..."

"Mike I been thinking, wouldn't it be a good idea to do somethin for ol John ... like how about a cut of the movie rights for his defense fund? ... I found out you got two million for the movie ..."

"We're thinking of doin something tomorrow night Abby-baby ... just hang on ..."

The rock group playing had just ended the set and seeing how the mike wasn't being used I sauntered up and in my black-leather acid voice shouted something at the People Hill like:

> The Politics of the event is Pot. Dig it! John Sinclair's in fuckin prison ten years for two fuckin joints. We ought to bust John out of prison or all this peace and music don't mean ...
> CLICK

Well I didn't give a shit if they cut the mike off. I got it out anyway. I wiped my nose and walked through the swarm of startled flower floaters crowding on the stage (third largest in the world no less). Everyone had this weird look with their eyes poppin out and their mouths hangin opened. It was sort of like I was their mother and just caught em jerking off ... God, here was Florence Nightingale passin out downers. I went to the corner and sat down on the edge of the stage, feeling pretty alone — and remembering when I was seventeen and pissed in my pants on the bus — everything was spinning for a while ... Mike came over and said, "What the fuck did you do that for??"

"Oh, I'm just doing my thing."

"Oh, O.K., come hear this group, they'll really blow your mind and calm down ... trust us Abby-baby ... we're with you all the way ..."

"Oh yeah, which band is playin?"

"The Who, that's who."

"The What?"

"No, man, The Who, from England, you know ..."

"Oh, yeah, The Who ... don't they bust their instruments?"

We sat on the stage listening to The Who tune up and all of a sudden I remembered ...

"Hey Mike, how you guys gonna make that pitch for John Sinclair tomorrow night? You said the festival was gonna end tomorrow afternoon ... you said you'd have the bands play right straight through and end it ..."

"Abbs-baby ... trust me ..."

"Mike, how can I trust Vanguard Capitalism? Why don't you make the announcement now before they play ..."

"Tomorrow, Abbs ..."

"Now Mike ..."

"Trust me, baby ..."

"Dare to struggle, dare to win, Mike baby!!!"

I lunged forward, grabbed the mike and shouted out "FREE JOHN SIN ..." (CRASH). Pete Townshend, lead guitarist, had clonked me over the head with his electric guitar, and I crumpled on the stage. There we were shaking fists at each other and yelling, him doing stuff like "Get the fuck outta here," and me doing the "You fascist pig" number. Then I turned to Mike ...

"That's a real bummer, Abbs-baby ..."

"Ah, fuck you Mike ... you're full of shit. Peace my ass, huh ... how come he tried to kill me? Don't forget about John Sinclair. I gotta get back to New York."

I leaped the chasm from the stage to the barricade wall, flying like some shaggy-dog Tarzan. I scrambled over the wall, leaped ten feet to the ground and started to climb People Hill. Past the rows and rows and rows of zonked-out people, higher and higher I climbed and the hill turned into Jacob's Ladder ...

> We are climbing Jacob's Ladder
> We are climbing Jacob's Ladder
> We are climbing Jacob's Ladder
> Nearer to the Lord.

143

The climb took me through mountains of beer cans and valleys of sleeping blankets, through oceans of paper plates and cross rivers of Pepsi Cola, up hills of Tootsie wrappers and through forests of incense and all the way peoplepeoplepeople more than I had ever seen in my whole life. At the top of the hill I turned to look at the stage. You had to squint to even see it, nestled down there in the valley of garbage and people. I could hear The Who finishin up with what seemed like "God Save the Queen ..." I kicked the mud off my boots, opened my fly and pissed long and good ... the yellow river turned to blue and green and worked its way through the forests of incense and around the hills of Tootsie wrappers and disappeared into the Pepsi Cola river.

I staggered into the Groovy Forest crying for my best friend, "Marty, Marty ..." Over to Movement City past Walter Teague who was stretching his muscles ready to take on the Marines in Khe Sanh, ready to plant the Vietcong flag on the top of the concession stand ...

"Marty ... Marty ..."

Past the free food tent where I dumped everything out of my pockets and threw off my leather jacket ...

"Marty ... Marty ..."

Back through the wooden sculpture playground where a guy was crying out:

Acid, acid, real Owsley Purple ...
Three bucks a cap ... Get em while they last ...

"Marty ... Marty ... Marty ... Marty ..."

Past the couple fuckin on the American flag in the trunk of the Oldsmobile on the side of the road.

"Marty ..."

Past a guy with old-fashioned clothes and a little growth, playing on a guitar, and croonin, "It's all right Ma, I'm only dyin." On and on until I staggered into a pink-and-white tent with a sign that said HOS-PITAL and collapsed on the cot murmuring

Blue ... Blue ... Blue Suede Shit ...

Good ol Ron, one of the only guys I can really trust, stared into my psychedelic eyes and shook his head. "Heard you were having a bad acid trip. Wanna go home?"

I just wheezed a little and flopped my arms ...

A funny-lookin guy in a white jumpsuit and a cowboy hat with a hole in the front came by and held my hand ...

"Who are you sonny?(!) WHAT is your name! (?) WHO are you?"

"WHO-WHO-WHO," said the owl lying face-down on the cot ...

The whole tent started to spin like a carousel and I flew round and round, round and pink and round and white and round ... Just then I saw her — vaguely at first and then clearer and clearer. God! She was beautiful. A long wisp of a creamy thing with straight black hair down to her ass and long eyelashes that fluttered when she perked her thin ghost-like lips. She looked like she just stepped out of a door in the *New York Times* Magazine Section with legs like the sleek '55 Corvette I used to race at dragstrips. She was all decked out in the most mini of minis, a silver see-through thingie, and she had no underwear on at all. She sat on the edge of the cot and started running her fingers through my hair. My left arm weighed a ton but I managed to get it up a little and aim it towards that valley under the Rim of the Silver Mini ... right where her crotch must have been ... I was almost there when her hand flicked my arm away ... lightly but firmly. She fluttered her eyelashes and pouted in a long, slim voice:

"Honey, you know what?"

"No, what ..." I was able to utter.

"You've come a long way, baby ..."

"Soooo .... let's ...... f .... u .... c .... k," I managed.

"But you've still got a long way to go."

... and WHAT died ....

One More Time, Baby

Well, I'm comin down now; the acid is wearing off. Slowly but surely I'm leaving the WOODSTOCK NATION and passing through the territory which surrounds our land — their world, the Nation of Pigs. It's reassuring that nothing much works out here either in the same way lots of things didn't work up there. The other night on the news Con Edison announced it just avoided another major black-out, the phone company apologized for not being able to complete any calls. They showed lines almost as long as the lines leading to WOODSTOCK NATION at golf courses around the city, commuters were screaming at the Long Island Rail Road and some military expert was glumly confessing that the Pigs had in fact been defeated in Vietnam. There was also a neat little item about a guy who was pissed at his lousy job and blew up a section of the Marine Midland Trust Bank in downtown Manhattan.... Seems as if maybe good ol George Metesky was back in business again and with George doing his thing, anything could happen. In a way, it's good to be back. It's good to know I can still write an album in five days when I thought I'd need at least six when I started. It's good to write the last of the closing songs cause this album was nothing but a bunch of beginnings and endings. I guess you figured out that I had mixed feelings about what happened up there in those few hectic days. Mostly about the cats who were running the show, some about myself, but none about the folks who worked and played together in WOODSTOCK NATION. When I think about it now, maybe it wouldn't have been such a bad place to live after all ... not a bad place to run around setting up hospitals and playing in the lake with my kids. Maybe it wouldn't have been a bad place to do all that groovy stuff ... maybe AFTER THE REVOLUTION. After, you say? That's right, after ... cause for me anyway there's still a long way to go ... lots of things to do. Take Woodstock, New York for example. Not the one you went to, the other one in PIG NATION where Bob Dylan really lives. Up in that Woodstock the cops don't wear scarlet jackets and smoke pot in the haystacks with teeny-boppers. Up in that Woodstock they belt you with a club if you sit down on the bench in the center of town. Up in that Woodstock last night they busted twenty-four people, including some mothers for pot, and are holding them on $120,000 bail. Up in that Woodstock they closed the public swimming places this summer just to keep the hippies out. Up in that Woodstock they cut your hair when they arrest you. Dig that, Samson of the Tulips! You gonna make that V-sign when some Pig shaves your head in the other Woodstock? Dig it Samson, we gotta build an Army to defend WOOD-STOCK NATION. Dig it Samson, we got to help free our brothers and sisters in prison. We can beat those motherfuckers, we can beat those Pigs, man ... all we gotta do is spread the word for next summer ... let's go up to Woodstock ... yeah, I hear that's where Bob Dylan lives ... I hear The Band will be out in the town square and Tim Hardin too ... I hear even The Who is coming up ... Wow! and it's all gonna be FREE, free up front ... and there'll be more of us than ever ... it'll be the biggest of all the festivals, bigger than Monterey, bigger than Atlantic City, bigger than Chicago, bigger than even White Lake itself .. it'll be the biggest fuckin free ROCK FESTIVAL of all. Only this time, yeah, groovy, this time we'll bring our own ROCKS ... just in case we need em ... it's time we brought the festival home to PIG NATION. Right on, Brother!

Biography

Abbie Hoffman has been called many things by many people, "Lenin of the Flower Children," "A Cross Between Lenny Bruce, Che Guevara and Robin Hood," "Biggest Ego-Tripper in the Country," and "Fucking Communist Bastard." After being thrown out of public school in Worcester, Massachusetts, for hitting his English teacher, he hustled pool for about a year until his parents decided to send him to a private school. Somehow he managed to finish and ended up at Brandeis University. There he studied under such men as Herbert Marcuse, Abraham Maslow, and Maurice Stein. He went to graduate school in psychology at the University of California at Berkeley and was a psychologist at Worcester State Hospital for two years.

In 1962 he went to work for the Stuart Hughes campaign for senator. Hughes was the first major peace candidate to run for a high office; his chief campaign pledge called for an end to nuclear testing. After the Hughes campaign Abbie became active in the civil rights movement. He worked for the Student Non-Violent (now National) Coordinating Committee, establishing Friends of SNCC groups around New England, and for CORE as community organizer in Massachusetts. From 1964 to 1966, he worked in various civil rights projects in the South, especially in Mississippi and Georgia. He was active in the Mississippi Freedom Party challenge at the Democratic National Convention in 1964 at Atlantic City, worked in a freedom school in McComb, Mississippi, and on voter registration in Americus, Georgia. In 1965, he went to work for the Poor People's Corporation of Mississippi, a network of People's Craft Cooperatives throughout the state. In 1966, he founded the first of many Liberty Houses in New York City to serve as retail outlets for the Cooperatives.

The winter of 1966 saw the emergence of a new culture in San Francisco, the Lower East Side of New York, and other metropolitan areas. Drugs, rock music, long hair, freaky clothes, free stores, Be-Ins, theatre-in-the-streets, bust-trusts, all played a part. Abbie worked on the first Be-Ins, Smoke-Ins (marijuana), established the first Free Store in New York, organized the Food Drive for Newark during the riots, and became perhaps the chief architect of the hippy movement in the East. He married Anita Kushner in June of 1967 in a hippy ceremony in

Central Park. He developed an action-theory of theatrical politics influenced by Antonin Artaud, Marshall McLuhan and Andy Warhol. Throwing money out at the Stock Exchange, dumping soot and smoke bombs in Con Edison's lobby, appearing naked in a church, and planting trees in the center of city streets were some of the best-known guerrilla theater events.

In August of 1967 he met Jerry Rubin, who encouraged him to play a role in the March on the Pentagon. He and others worked out a scenario for the "Exorcism of the Pentagon" and helped bring people to Washington. A number of street demonstrations followed, culminating in the founding of the Yippies and the Festival of Life at the Democratic Convention in Chicago. Since then he has been hounded by "neanderthal forces in the Pig power structure," including the F.B.I., Chicago and New York Police Intelligence divisions, local cops, HUAC, and the courts. Ten of his forty arrests have occurred since Chicago, but the troubles with the police and courts have produced theatrics of their own, an example of which was his trial for wearing a Flag Shirt to the HUAC hearings. This case is currently on appeal in the Washington District Court of Appeals.

He is the author of numerous articles in the underground press under a variety of pseudonyms. He also authored *Fuck the System* (given out free) and the controversial *Revolution for the Hell of It* (Dial Press). He considers himself a cultural revolutionary and believes violence is inevitable in the clash between the emerging culture and the dying one. He believes that the culture should be defended by any means necessary, including use of self-defensive violence.

For more information see *Revolution for the Hell of It* and the files of the Federal Bureau of Investigation.

Epilogue

Epologue

The Head Withers
as Body Grows

Somewhere deep inside the bowels of the monster born in Bethel also lay the kernel for its destruction. Perhaps it was the egocentric greed of the Rock Empire itself. Maybe it was the strain of cannibalism inherited from our parents and exaggerated when cramped into railroad flats in the slums or on muddy slopes in front of gargantuan stages. The rapes, the bad acid burns, stealing from each other, they, too, were part of the Woodstock experience, if not the Nation. Smack and speed didn't help. "Shooting up" is more than just a casual expression. It is symbolic of the suicidal death trip, the frustration, the despair. It is another way to bring the apocalypse a little closer.

Janis was the heroine of Woodstock

Nation. Bold and sassy, her energy could ignite millions. I saw her perform all over the country. In the funky old Aragon Ballroom in Chicago, in the Fillmores West and East, on TV, backstage where she would line up a row of twenty studs, in the Chelsea Hotel bar and on the street. She used to drop into our place at all sorts of weird hours when we lived around the corner from the Fillmore East. She was the only person I ever saw use a needle. When she popped in a load and pulled out the works, she'd cluck her tongue making a sucking noise and her face would break out into that shit-eating grin like the one I run down dedicating this book to Lenny Bruce. The very thought of it makes me shiver. You couldn't know Janis without knowing her death was near and you couldn't know the Rock Empire without knowing her death would mean a bundle to the horde of enterprising vultures who choose to pick at the corpse.

Perhaps if I had stayed through Sunday at the festival I would have experienced Jimi Hendrix. Folks told me his rendition of "The Star-Spangled Banner" was in the same spirit that I wore the flag shirt to Congress. They said that Jimi desecrated and defiled the symbols of Amerika because he abhorred its basic corruptness —a feeling difficult to maintain on fifty-thousand-dollar-a-night performances. Jimi Hendrix was the only rock performer I know of who gave bread to anything most of us would call "radical." It's possible that some others gave to projects out in California, especially in the heyday of Haight-Ashbury, but as far as the things I came in contact with, only Jimi gave. He laid some bread on us for the Trial in Chicago and footed most of the bill for a certain marijuana mail-out alluded to in this book. Now he's dead too, same as Janis, and the rest of the Rock Empire rolls on. "Just keep pushing the myth forward," yell the makeup men and groupies. And the walls around the stars get higher and electric fences and police dogs guard their mansions.

The last time I saw Jimi was just before he performed at a West Village benefit for Tim Leary when Tim was still conning everyone into thinking he loved jail and everything like that while he planned his escape. I was pissing mad. Cambodia had been invaded; Kent State, Jackson and Augusta had occurred. That afternoon I had been at the New York City Strike Control Center at Pace College. The place was being guarded like an armed fort. For the past few days, squads of hard hats with blackjacks and meat hooks had raided the school, making mincemeat out of students. The sight of young kids with long ugly gashes in their skin and stitches in their scalps was awful scary. Reports of police cheering on the goons echoed the dawning of street fascism. The cries of the wounded rang in my ears as we made our way to the Village Gate. What relationship did the scene at Pace College have to the upcoming gala benefit ($25 a head)? How many Woodstock Nations were there?

We arrived early and camped in a joint across the street with ample view of the arriving limousines with rent-a-chauffeurs and fastidiously feathered rock and dope-dealing aristocrats. The sight of hippies disembarking from Cadillac limousines does not sit well in the belly of a cultural revolutionary.

During the Trial, Anita and I were granted an audience in the court of Mick Jagger I in the dressing room of the Chicago International Amphitheater. When we left the sacred chamber, a stockily built man about forty-eight in a chauffeur's suit stopped us and smiled. "Abbie, I'm Mick's private chauffeur," he said. "My name's Al." We chatted trial-gossip for awhile waiting for the performance to begin and then Al dropped the clunker. "It's really a small world. You know who I chauffeur during the day???" He paused to suck me in real good and lowered the boom. "Judge Julius Hoffman!" That chauffeur in Chicago probably knew more than Buddha.

Anyways, you can see why the line of limousines didn't cheer me up none. We're all sitting around the table bullshitting and drinking our root beer and LSD floats when Blood, Sweat & Tears sitting at the next table leans back and enters the conversation. "Hey, man, guess what? We're bringing our revolution behind the iron curtain next month. Ain't it a gas?" Now

160

the phrase, "behind the iron curtain" doesn't really jive with the phrase "our revolution" and we all lean forward getting curiouser by the minute. "Yeah, man, we're getting $60,000 to tour Eastern Europe and the CIA is footing the bill." Our shock is interpreted as admiration and BS & T continue. "That isn't all, we're doing a benefit to establish four scholarship funds for the four students shot." The shock waves begin to jell into a group numbness. Anita breaks the spell, "Doesn't it seem inappropriate to raise money for scholarships in the name of four kids who died trying to close the school?" BS & T is annoyed. In their world, women are not supposed to speak unless spoken to, never mind question their wisdom. "Listen, honey," chimes BS & T, "in the fall the strike will be over and the school will be back in session. There are some deserving kids that need a chance." At that point I let loose a shower of saliva which caused a lot of shoving and yelling. A week later we stormed Madison Square Garden, where they were performing, with red, white and blue signs reading "BLOOD, SWEAT AND BULLSHIT—the CIA's Top Group" and threw twenty pounds of shit in the main aisle to emphasize the point.

Woodstock without any politics, without a commitment to self-defense of the Nation is a shuck. A tin-pan alley rip-off. When they say, "Hey, man, politics is not where it's at," what they are really saying is, "Don't bug me, I wanna keep all my dough and the status quo." Peter Max is Consciousness III. Peter Max loves the planet earth. Peter Max paints designs for bathtowels sold by gas stations across the country that pollute that very planet. That whole scene of hip fashions is not the scene of this book. Woodstock Nation is not the Woodstock movie. Woodstock Nation is at war with the Pig Empire; the Woodstock movie is a weapon in the arsenal of the pigs, designed to defeat the Nation by rendering it impotent. People at Warner Brothers brag how they purged the Nation from the movie. Most of the stuff in this book ended up on the cutting room floor.

Now we are in heavy times. The post-Altamont blues have set in. Scag has come to town. People stab each other. Rock is dead. Folks say The Revolution is over. Winter is longer now. Ecology freaks debate if there are five or ten years left on earth. By the fall, when this book comes out, the trend will be "the New Nostalgia," sounds of the fifties will be in, funky movies, maybe even suede shoes . . . it will be the fifties of Pat Boone and Dwight Eisenhower, of apathy and body drugs. Trends are made in the cities and Woodstock Nation has abandoned the cities as smoldering cesspools.

Woodstock Nation ain't dead at all. In fact, when the hip profiteers clean up the songs, rediscover the fact that pornography is safer than politics, we'll all be better off. Woodstock Nation's got real roots. In Vermont, Santa Barbara, New Mexico, Florida, Kansas and all over. Millions upon millions of young people are choosing the new culture. As Jerry Rubin says, "We Are Everywhere." Not only here but all around the world. The division in culture is so real you can reach out and touch it. The Oedipal Conflict has replaced Marxian Dialectics as revolutionary politics in a post-scarcity economy. There are generation struggles in unions, in churches, in the army. As I write, high schools in Boston have been closed for three weeks because of fighting. There have been fires set and bombs exploded. All young people are not Weathermen, but no young person would ever squeal on a fugitive without being branded a traitor. That is the Woodstock Nation. On television last night scenes of South Vietnamese puppet soldiers fleeing back across the border at the hands of the Pathet-lao and the North Vietnamese appeared. Young people cheered "the enemy." That is the Woodstock Nation. There is no community in the land without a vast number of communes, food conspiracies, alternate universities, violent underground, dope-dealing networks, people's rock groups, switchboards and newspapers. That is the Woodstock Nation. Growing roots of authentic life in the plastic land of death is not easy. But it's happening. Don't believe me, Eric Sevareid or Charles Reich or the

East Village Other or **Life** Magazine or anybody. We're all a bunch of liars. Go out and see for yourself.

Abbie Hoffman
March 10, 1971